Rare Imperial Glass Patterns

Myrna Garrison

Schiffer Publishing Ltd
4880 Lower Valley Road, Atglen, Pennsylvania 19310

Dedication

In Memory of Bob Garrison, 1927-2006

The book is dedicated to the memory of a wonderful husband and father. For fity-eight years, we had a great time doing things we enjoyed: being with family, having company, sharing our glass collecting, traveling, and enjoying our home together. To quote our favorite song, *Too Young*, "This love will last though years may go."

Without hesitation, Bob put his family first. The times our children joined us at NIGCS conventions were special for us. They were proud of their father and they made him proud of them. There was mutual admiration with his grandchildren. He enjoyed building things for us and our family. When asked for one word that described what they had learned from their dad, Janna and Robert both answered, "integrity."

Bob loved everything about our glass collecting: the trips, seminars, displays, research, books, and most of all the friends we made.

The dedication of this book would be incomplete without including our special family: our son Robert and his wife Jenny; our daughter Janna and her husband Kirkby, and our four grandchildren: Kendra, Nathan, Matthew, and Scott. Bob and I shared many holidays and special occasions with them. Before they married, we had Church events, Scouts, band trips, camping trips, and automobile adventures. After they married, they continued to include us in all phases of their lives. We gathered on ski slopes, cruise ships, and foreign land in addition to the usual family gatherings. They continue to be there for me and plan things for me to do with them.

Other Schiffer Books by Myrna and Bob Garrison:
Candlewick: Colored and Decorated Lines
Candlewick: The Crystal Line
Imperial Cape Cod Glass
Milk Glass: Imperial Glass Corporation

Photographs by Myrna & Bob Garrison

Library of Congress Control Number: 2008927599

Covers and book designed by Bruce Waters
Type set in Huminest 521 BT

ISBN: 978-0-7643-2984-5
Printed in China

Published by Schiffer Publishing Ltd.
4880 Lower Valley Road
Atglen, PA 19310
Phone: (610) 593-1777; Fax: (610) 593-2002
E-mail: Info@schifferbooks.com

In Europe, Schiffer books are distributed by
Bushwood Books
6 Marksbury Ave.
Kew Gardens
Surrey TW9 4JF England
Phone: 44 (0) 20 8392-8585; Fax: 44 (0) 20 8392-9876
E-mail: info@bushwoodbooks.co.uk
Website: www.bushwoodbooks.co.uk
Free postage in the U.K., Europe; air mail at cost.

Acknowledgements

Bob and I worked diligently on this book until the last six months he lived. During his last months, work on the book was not feasible. We spent his remaining time sharing many wonderful visits from family and friends.

We thought the book was about 90% finished, but I found out that was not quite right. Bob and I had photographed most of the items we had at home. Bev and Jim Harris brought some of their special items to be photographed. After the 2005 National Imperial Glass Convention, we came by the Harris's home in Missouri and photographed some more. While there, we also photographed the rare animals that Todd Harris has collected.

When I did finally bring the book out and start working on it again, I had several offers of help. Beverly and Jim Harris stepped forward and encouraged me to let them help. It was difficult to accept their offer because it has always been "our" efforts. Bev and Jim proofread and checked mould numbers, color names, etc. If they had different ideas on a number, color, or price, that would be put down. The red ink flowed. All of this was made more difficult because they had no pictures to compare with the captions. We kept large sections of material going through the internet—what a wonderful means to do this it is. Indeed, what a lot of laughs we have had. There are not enough words to thank them for their effort.

My thanks go also to David Cleveland, who has been supportive in many ways. He helped me with glass, errands, airport runs, and everything else that I needed. He called often and checked to see what more he could do. I knew that I could call him to help me anytime.

There are still others who helped in various ways. Some priced, others shared glass, many asked when the book would be finished, and others have given me support, visits, and telephone calls. I owe a lot to these special friends: Kathy Burch, Max Miller, Keith Burkart, Paul Gould, Shirley and Art Moore, Ruth and David Adkisson, Norma Boren, Kevin Kiley, Paul and Judy Douglas, and Mike and Mary Lee Wilson, Dick and Pat Spencer, Beverly Lester, and many non-glass friends.

My thanks go to Walt Lemiski for a long-distance friendship. He contacted me after he had reviewed our first Schiffer book, *Milk Glass: Imperial Glass Corporation*. Soon he was working on his own book, *Elegant Glass with Corn Flower*. After an exchange of many e-mails, he came to the Imperial Convention so we could meet. That was a very special occasion. Walt has an interesting, wonderful background-- teaching, writing, and singing to name only a few of his abilities. Be sure you read his Foreword to our book for the wonderful analogy of a musical genius and the Imperial Glass Corporation. He may have overstated the comments about the Garrisons, but he certainly hit it right about Imperial Glass. Thanks, Walt.

To Nancy Schiffer a mere thank you is not enough for the time and effort it took to input my corrections in the galley proofs.

My thanks also to Peter Schiffer, who has been patient and supportive. His telephone calls have been reassuring and helpful. Peter is responsible for encouraging us to write the Candlewick books that we had always wanted to write. He is also responsible for urging us to tackle this book of lesser-known patterns. His confidence in us has been gratifying.

Foreword

The famous Russian composer Sergei Rachmaninov (1873-1943) was known to most everyone in his day for his "Prelude in C-sharp Minor," written in 1892. This little gem of a piano work captivated the public and was Rachmaninov's first popular success. However, it was just one of a set of Thirteen Preludes from his Opus 3. Rachmaninov's audiences could not get enough of "The Prelude," and would not let him leave the stage until he had performed it. He came to loath this little piece. After all, Rachmaninov was the composer of piano concertos, symphonies, operas, choral music, piano pieces, and chamber works. Despite his very substantial catalog of musical works, the public knew him for that Prelude!

Less high-brow composers are sometimes remembered as one-hit wonders, often despite a large body of other compositions. The prolific pop music composer and singer, Eric Carmen, is known to most folks as the writer of "All By Myself," from 1976. Coincidentally, this melody was derived from a snippet of Sergei Rachmaninov's "Second Piano Concerto." Rachmaninov might well have commiserated with Carmen.

If the Imperial Glass Company were a composer, one could imagine that it would have been similar in stature to Rachmaninov, having produced a large diverse body of superior quality works. Imperial undoubtedly would also have intensely disliked being remembered solely for just one of its lines, Candlewick. Most Americans, when they can remember the name of that beaded pattern, would probably say, "Oh yeah, Imperial made Candlewick glassware." While that one phenomenal pattern, Imperial's No. 400 Candlewick line, is an incredible and massive opus, it did tend to draw attention away from numerous other works, overshadowing many of Imperial's amazing creations.

All glass collectors know the story of Candlewick; some know quite a bit about Cape Cod; Carnival glass collectors know about Imperial's production of iridescent glassware; others know about the Lace Edge line. These were all substantial Imperial Glass Company endeavors. They have been covered quite thoroughly by capable glass researchers. But what of all those dozens and dozens of smaller patterns? What of all those special order items produced specifically for other companies? What about lamps and lighting fixtures, art glass, hand-painted pieces, and all the other unique items?

Selections from vintage Imperial Glass catalogs (1904 to 1934) chosen by authors Margaret and Douglas Archer for their 1978 publication *Imperial Glass Company* served to whet collectors' appetites for diverse Imperial items. The catalogue pages show a wide variety of glass shapes, sizes, and styles. The monumental three-volume *Encyclopedia of Imperial Glass*, edited by James Measell and produced between 1995 and 1999, served to open the door on so much more of Imperial's glass production. With the door ajar on the vast range of Imperial wares, a marvelous thing happened...many more questions were asked and more details were begging to be filled in.

Myrna Garrison is one of the most thorough, detailed, and precise researchers whose books one might ever have the good fortune to read. She has an uncanny knack of being able to illuminate incredible details. She also has a wonderful habit of expanding captions far beyond the mere basic details into delightful flights of valuable information.

I was most fortunate to have the cooperation of the crack Garrison team during my own research and scribbling; I would turn to the dynamic duo of Bob and Myrna when searching for Imperial answers. What Myrna might not know at the drop of a hat, Bob would patiently unearth through delving into the Garrison's extensive paper archives. Seldom did my mysteries ever go unsolved, as precious research materials were unreservedly shared.

You are surely bound to revel in this sharing of yet more of the wealth of information now revealed about Imperial Glass Company's wares. The Garrisons have busily been presenting much of their findings for years at glass conventions across the nation. Even with their full schedule and wonderfully jam-packed presentations, it would take more than a lifetime to share all their knowledge. Thank goodness they also share this with us in print, since the breadth of Imperial's production is truly both staggering and sensational --from what was one of America's greatest glass producers.

Walter T. Lemiski, Director
Canadian Depression Glass Association

Contents

Guide To Using This Book

The main purpose of this book is to bring to the attention of Imperial Glass collectors the wide variety of Imperial's production. Many of us have only studied the one pattern interest that we have. Eventually most of us become interested in another phase of Imperial. We wanted to share a few of the smaller pattern lines and groups of items that we have found interesting. This book does not attempt to give complete information; it only opens a door to invite you to come in and find something different.

It is just as important to read what has been said about the item as well as to study the photographs. We have attempted to put pertinent information in each caption but often much more is needed to tell the story. When necessary, that is presented in the text before the photographs. Remember that when we give a listing of items, we will first list the mould number and then the description. Other information will be included when useful.

Numbering System

Prefix numbers will generally indicate the pattern line. The numbers to the right of the forward diagonal are numbers assigned by Imperial to specify the particular identification of the individual item. Often the only number given is the general pattern number. A few times Imperial changed the identification number during the production years of the piece. This is confusing to researchers and collectors, but it is something that has to be accepted. In presenting the different items, we will generally list them in numerical order according to items within a group. If we have an item in a pattern for which we have not found a catalog number for identification, we will place the pattern number in parenthesis.

In 1973, Lenox changed Imperial's numbering system to a five-digit number. For the few pieces that are shown that were made in the Lenox era, we did not attempt to give a dual number. For ease of reference, we used the original numbers.

Letter Symbols for Shapes

Imperial used letters after the designated item number for design information. In factory paper, there was a list of "Symbols for Shapes." We are including it the way it appeared on the paper we have. This is not presumed to be a complete list. Some day you may be studying another pattern and one of the letters will answer a question.

A Round
B Bowl
C Crimped
D Flat plate
E Turned-up handles or sides
F Float or shallow bowl
H Heart or fancy crimp
J Slight outward roll at top
L Rolled over and out
N Slight inward roll at top
R Rolled over and down
S Square
TB Tid bit
V Plate with cupped edge
X Not on the symbol's list but has been interpreted to mean Flat Rim

In looking at the charts and working on this part, we found it interesting that most of the use of the letters occurred in items made in the late 1930s and early 1940s. Fewer letters were used in the later mould numbers and then only when those numbers are sets. We cannot guess at what formula Imperial used in its numbering of items.

Imperial sometimes used different words as names for the same items through the eighty-year life of Imperial production. It would be difficult to attempt to use all of those names on every item; it would be confusing and cumbersome. We will use the name that appeared most often in catalogs that collectors are most likely to see. To explain this better, consider comporte and compote, candlestick and candleholder, partitioned and divided, and nappy and bowl. Although in today's usage the word "ashtray" is generally written as one word, we have used it as two words since that is the way Imperial wrote the word in all of its catalogs. We have attempted to project all information as nearly as Imperial did for the sake of Imperial history.

Pronunciation of words is another variable with which we have struggled. Spelling is sometimes confusing. Imperial spelled mould both with and without the "u." In the past, we generally used the spelling "mold" because that was the most often used spelling by Imperial. However, in this book we decided to use mould when referring to the iron vessel the molten glass was poured into for shaping the products.

Two words come to mind that we hear pronounced in different ways, e.g. Stiegel and Verde. We have checked with other sources and find these explanations: Stiegel, a word of German extraction, is pronounced with the first "e" as a long "e." Another word is Verde, Italian extraction, is pronounced with the first "e" short, and the second "e" long.

Measurements

Measurements given by Imperial in its description of items sometimes refer to the height and sometimes refer to the width. Always remember that hand-made glass measurements can vary in size.

Dates

In our previous books, we built charts in order to be able to give the first and last dates of production that we could find. However, for this book, we have only given approximate dates because so many records have been lost over the years. We have little printed material to work with in the 1940s and 1950s. Interestingly, Candlewick, Cape Cod and Milk Glass all had specialized catalogs through the years. These catalogs helped to establish the dates of productions. In this book, the subjects are generally short in production time and with only general references, dates are difficult to determine. Our resources for the 1930s are very limited and sometimes undated, and therefore, any dates involving that period are subject to challenge. When a date is not shown, it is generally because the factory information available to us was not dated.

Glass-making Definitions

We will attempt to explain one feature that puzzles all collectors. Items sometimes have a raised ridge on the underneath of the piece. Some of the same pieces will not have this but instead will have a ground and polished bottom. When the items have the extra ridge of glass that one can take hold of, it is called a marie. A marie is on a snapped-up item. A ground and polished item has been "stuck-up" on a puntie rod. According to "A Consumer and Retail Guide to Handcrafted Glassware":

To fire polish and/or change the shape of an item it is attached to one of two types of rod-like iron tools: A "puntie" or a "snap." The face or surface of a puntie is red hot, and newly formed glass will easily attach itself to the hot iron [hence the term, stuck-up].

A snap, however, is a long rod with moveable jaws on one end. The jaws on the snap open to grip the glass item. After being mounted on a snap or puntie, the glass item is placed into a small furnace called a "glory hole." The item heats up, becomes quite soft, and must be spun to maintain its shape. The "finisher" now shapes the item with a charred wooden tool. Oak or apple wood is used, since neither contains rosin, which could seriously mark the glass.

Fire polishing is done for two reasons: first, to give the surface of the glass a higher brilliancy, and second, to soften the glass if it requires a final shaping.

After finishing, the item is detached from either the snap or the *puntie*, and placed in a Lehr (annealing oven) to be tempered. Snapped-up items require no further processing after annealing, while items stuck-up must be ground and polished after annealing to remove any rough edges remaining on the foot or base of an item that has stuck to the *puntie*.

Sometimes the *marie* bottom was the early design, on other items the ground and polished bottom was the early version. It cannot be stated that marie bottoms are all the early style. The only time that Imperial indicated the ground and polished bottoms in price lists was on plates. Marie bottoms were not specifically mentioned.

Crack off is the excess glass that every piece of blown ware has. An item must be shaped so that it can be inflated to completely fill the mould and assume the proper shape. After annealing, it is necessary to "crack off" the unwanted cap or top portion of the glass. The glass is scored by a wheel, then a hot flame is applied to the scored mark and the unwanted glass will crack off along the scratch. The resulting rough edge is sharp and uneven and must be ground smooth.

Answers to Often-asked Questions

What you always wanted to know but did not have access to all of the answers. This section is dedicated to telling it like Imperial told it to its retail customers. The following paper is not dated, but it does contain clues to an approximate date.

What is the difference between blowing and pressing glass?

Blowing, the oldest method of forming glass, is done with the aid of an iron blowpipe by a skilled glass worker. Molten glass is gathered on the end of a blowpipe; it is then removed from the glass pot somewhat cooled, carefully shaped, and then the glob of glass is blown (by means of the mouth and lungs) into a hollow body. The blower shapes the glass bubble further, and in most cases, blows it into the shape in the mold.

Hand pressed glassware is distinguished from blown glassware by the fact that in pressing, both the inside and outside surfaces of the article are formed and shaped by a mold, in pressed glassware the pressure being exerted by an iron former or plunger instead of just lung power alone, as in blowing. A pressed article can finally be hand-shaped in the same manner as a blown article, by a skilled finisher using wooden, carbon, or other types of hand tools.

Both methods, pressing and blowing, require highly skilled workmen. Too, a pressed article can be finally hand shaped in the same manner as a blown article: by a skilled finisher using wooden, carbon, or other types of hand tools.

How is glass cut?

Cut glass is glass decorated with various patterns which are cut into the surface of the glass. The first step is to lay out and mark onto the surface of the glass a skeleton of the pattern to be cut. The glass surface is then cut into with an abrasive cutting wheel until the desired effect is achieved. In some cases the design is left in its original gray texture; in others, the cut design is polished with cork wheels or by a polishing process utilizing acid, until the whole design sparkles with the same brilliancy as the uncut surface of the glass.

Where do the raw materials for the glass come from and what are they?

The raw materials that go into glass come from a

variety of geographical locations: sand comes from New Jersey, Pennsylvania and Illinois. Soda ash is made from salt. Though once imported, potash is now supplied to Imperial domestically. The special salts from which potash is made come from California, Texas, New Mexico, and other states. Nitrate of Soda and Nitrate of Potash are manufactured chemically from raw materials, but are also obtainable as natural minerals. Borax is a refined natural mineral. Lime, made from limestone, comes from Missouri, Northern Ohio and Northeastern Pennsylvania.

How is colored glass made?

Colored glass is made by adding various elements to the basic glass batch. Ruby or red glass is generally made by adding Metallic Selenium and Sulphide of Cadmium to the glass "batch." Chrome Oxide or Chrome and Cobalt Oxides will make green glass. Copper and Cobalt Oxides will color glass blue. Nickel will color glass gray. Iron will color glass brown or green, depending on how the chemicals are used. So as you can see, various mixtures will give glass various tints, just like mixing different colors of paint to achieve a desired effect. [The word "red" has been found only a few times in Imperial written work. This may be one of four times referenced in this book.]

How long has glass been made?

The early Egyptians, some thousands of years ago, are credited with first using glass—as a coating or glaze for pottery. Glass, of itself, was not even made into beads, undoubtedly the first all-glass product, until about 5,000 years ago. And not until 1500 B.C. was it discovered that vessels could be made of glass. There still exists, in fact, a handmade glass goblet, over 3500 years old, used by Thut-Mose III, King of Egypt.

What are Imperial's molds made from?

All of the molds used at Imperial Glass are made of a special cast iron alloy known for its extremely fine crystalline structure and high heat resistance. The designs are worked into the molds by means of a hammer and chisel. However, all of the designs are "sculpted" into the molds in reverse of the design wanted on the glass. Final polishing of a mold is done with small, handmade files that enable the mold maker to create very intricate detailing, such as that found on our Cape Cod and Collectors Crystal patterns.

How is slag glass made?

"Slag Glass" or "End O'Day Glass" is a years-old, original creation of the glass workers themselves, who at the end of a work day, would combine milk glass with a colored glass to produce the unique "marble effect." No two pieces of slag glass are alike, and each reflects the individuality of the glassworker. Imperial creates Jade Slag—shades of turquoise green with white milk glass: Caramel Slag—deep rich caramel hues with traditional milk glass; and "Ruby" Slag, the ultimate in slag glass—combines bright ruby glass with milk glass. The vibrant reds and fiery colors are created by reheating the item after it is hand formed.

Is Imperial glass dishwasher and refrigerator safe?

Imperial Glass tableware is made to withstand normal daily use. With proper care it can be used for hot as well as cold foods. Technically, it is not heat resistant and will not withstand abrupt temperature changes. Nothing hot should be put into crystal that has been chilled. Don't put glasses that have contained ice immediately into hot water. Warm them gradually by rinsing first.

Imperial glass can be cleaned in an automatic dishwasher. However, like all fine glass, its brilliancy will eventually become dulled by the detergent.

Hand-wash glass in clean, pleasantly hot water and light suds. A little water softener in the water will add to the item's brilliancy. Never use strong soaps or scalding water on decorated crystal.

With proper care, your customer's Imperial glassware will retain its brilliancy, clarity and beauty for many, many years.

How do I tell cut glass from etched glass?

Cut Glass is glass decorated with patterns which are actually cut into the surface of the glass with an abrasive cutting wheel. The cut pattern stands out because it is deeply carved into the surface of the glass.

To etch the surface of glass with a design or pattern, the glass is coated with an acid-resisting solution, leaving uncoated only that part which is to be the eventual design pattern. The glass article is next immersed in hydrofluoric acid for a period of time. The glass is then removed from the acid bath and washed thoroughly in hot water. During washing, the acid-resisting material comes off and the glass article emerges from the washing process with the design silvery etched or eaten into the surface of the glass.

How is glass frosted, such as the Slag Line?

Glass, such as Imperial's "Slag" line, is frosted by sand blasting. The sand blasting process consists of spraying an abrasive material, such as sand, onto the surface of the glass at high pressure and great speed. A glass article can be frosted all over by sand blasting to a silky satin finish or to a deep rough finish, depending on the time of exposure to the blast of sand and the coarseness of the sand blasting material.

What's Imperial's best-selling pattern(s)?

Imperial's best-selling tableware patterns are OLD WILLIAMSBURG and CAPE COD. Both patterns include tableware, stemware and accessories, with OLD WILLIAMSBURG offering stemware in a variety of colors.

OLD WILLIAMSBURG features Colonial styling in graceful crystal tableware and serving accessories. The pattern is an elegant and eloquent as the manor houses in which the originals were found. The classic, hand-pressed simplicity which makes OLD WILLIAMSBURG so memorable also makes it a delight to own or to give as a striking and appreciated gift.

Imperial's hand press CAPE COD pattern closely follows the earliest American designs, themselves imitations of earlier English cuttings. Authentically Early American, CAPE COD is a timeless favorite. Stemware, tumblers and tableware combine to give a hostess unlimited choices in setting everything from a Sunday Brunch to Afternoon Tea.

What's the difference between Imperial Glass and Libby or Anchor Hocking?

The major difference between Imperial and Libby or Anchor Hocking can be summed up in three words: handcrafted versus machine. At Imperial, virtually every step in the manufacturing process—from the handling of the raw material to the finished piece—is a hand operation. At machine glass companies, "mass production" reigns supreme. Companies such as Anchor Hocking can produce literally millions of pieces of glass a year, all looking the same, all weighing the same, and all created by a machine that obviously can take no pride in its work. At Imperial, our glassworkers are our most important asset. Because we are a "hand glass" house, the workers are craftsmen, masters at their trade, deeply involved in what they are doing. They take pride in producing a handcrafted product—one that is unique and one that requires a special blending of skills and artistry to produce: not just the push of a button to start up a machine.

What's so special about hand made glass?

What's so special about hand made glass is this: There is no substitute for the grace, beauty and artistic individuality that comes only from the fine handcraftsmanship of glass.

In a world dominated by mass production, Imperial Glass continues to create only handcrafted glassware. Pride of workmanship, skill, and a deep devotion to quality are the prime motivators of Imperial's dedicated glassmasters. The delicate touch of a man whose life is devoted to handcraftsmanship makes the creation of fine glass more than just a skill to be learned. Rather it is an art form reached only through the close relationship of body and mind.

As one of the few remaining craft industries in the U. S., Imperial is aware of the responsibilities of its proud heritage and we acknowledge that the American consumer does and should expect our product to be superior to all those competitive to it.

How long do the molds last?

The lifetime of a hand press glass mold is hard to determine precisely. It depends on how many individual parts the mold has that can wear out; how often the mold is used; the skill of the glassworker; and many other factors. At Imperial, some of the molds date back 50 years or more. However, because of the constant care and maintenance our molds receive, it's conceivable that they could still be in use 50 years from now.

How is Carnival Glass made?

A piece of Carnival Glass begins as a piece of brilliant, clear crystal, produced just as other Imperial crystal items are produced. What gives Carnival Glass its unique, lustrous, metallic iridescence is a special mixture of chemicals that is sprayed on the crystal at high speed while the glass is still hot from the mold. The chemical spray is imbedded in the hot crystal and when permanently fired-in, creates a piece of glass that sparkles with subtle high-lights of gentle iridescence.

What lines does Imperial produce?

Imperial Glass produces a variety of hand press glass items including stemware, tableware and accessories, giftware, and barware.

Tableware lines include CAPE COD, OLD WILLIAMSBURG, REVERE, and CANDLEWICK.

Hand pressed stemware patterns include OLD WILLIAMSBURG, HOFFMAN HOUSE, CAPE COD, and FLOWER FAIR.

Imperial offers three cut barware patterns, five gold decorated crystal barware patterns, plus matching accessories and a line of decanters.

Our GIFTWARE lines are varied and include:

1. Americana Items
2. Candleholders and Candelabras
3. Collectors Crystal
4. White and Rubigold Carnival Glass
5. Fired Gold on Crystal Items
6. Slag Glass in Ruby, Caramel, and Jade Green

[The items mentioned in this question all appear in the 1975-76 catalog.]

How is Milk Glass made?

Milk Glass is a mixture of the same raw materials that go into making regular glass. Milk Glass becomes Milk Glass simply by the addition of a special chemical to the basic glass batch. In other words, Milk Glass is made just as other colored glass is, the only difference being the color. [Notice the omission of that special chemical!]

Are bubbles in glass considered imperfections?

Bubbles in glass are not considered imperfections unless they are present in such numbers as to dull the clarity of the glass. Generally, bubbles are no more than very tiny air pockets trapped in the glass during pressing or blowing. More than anything, bubbles are an indication of hand crafting. They are less likely to appear in machine-made glass because of the mechanical exactness of production process. So though a bubble may seem to be an imperfection in a glass article, it is actually an indication of handcraftsmanship and the uniqueness of each individual piece of glass, rather than the soulless conformity of machine-made glass. [A certain number of bubbles was allowed to pass the hand inspection of finished glass. The number permitted has not been learned or found.]

What is lead crystal and what does the lead do for the crystal?

Briefly, lead crystal is crystal (or clear glass) to which a certain percentage of lead oxide has been added during the manufacturing process. For example, Waterford is lead crystal, as is Imperial's Candlewick goblet and annual Collector's Christmas Plate. All other items are unleaded.

In this country, crystal glass is defined as "clear, uncolored glass." At Imperial, our crystal is made to be the color of distilled water: that is, virtually colorless.

Lead is added to glass for several reasons. First and foremost, because it makes the crystal softer for cutting. You'll notice that all Waterford is cut crystal, never uncut. Imperial's unleaded crystal, however, is soft enough for cutting, although the only cut items we produce are barware and decanters. However, our glass is still soft enough, without lead to press exceptionally well.

Next, lead gives cut crystal more brilliancy AND CLARITY. However, lead in crystal makes very little difference otherwise, except for increasing the price of the piece. Leaded crystal is, as you know, generally more expensive than unleaded crystal.

Most imported lead crystal is labeled "24% lead," while much of domestic lead crystal contains no more than 12% lead. Although some lead crystal may contain as much as 33% lead, any high lead content will soften the glass too much, and give it a tendency toward cloudiness.

All in all, while some people attach a great importance to owning genuine lead crystal, we at Imperial feel that the quality and brilliance of our unleaded crystal, such as our Collectors Crystal, is comparable to almost any lead crystal sold in American retail stores.

What is a Pokal?

It is a mug, jug, or jar; a vessel for cooling wine or water; a large, usually covered, goblet typically made of glass or silver. A nappy? It is a shallow open serving dish sometimes having one handle.

What is a comporte?

A bowl shaped dish with a stem or foot and sometimes with a cover for holding fruits or sweets.

A spider?

A cast iron fry pan. [In the case of Cape Cod, it would be the glass shaped as a fry pan.]

Pricing

The prices in this book are just a guide. There has not been a great deal of buying and selling activity on many of the items in this book, so prices are difficult to suggest. The prices were compiled by using prices seen on pieces for sale in antique malls, shops, shows, and similar places in various locations. The prices do not reflect those very good low prices you find in those fun to search places nor do they reflect the exaggerated high prices that are sometimes seen in auctions of any type. An asterisk will be used when a piece is seldom presented for sale due to rarity. Prices are based on mint condition. Prices are per each item unless stated otherwise. NP means "not priced." The prices reflect what a knowledgeable buyer will pay a knowledgeable seller for an item. We say, "Judge a price by demand, desirability, and the availability."

A price guide is not intended to set prices. The authors and publisher do not assume any responsibility for losses that might be incurred by the use of the price guide.

In all pricing, we have shown an asterisk (*) if there is not enough activity on the item to establish a guide. Sets are not always the sum of the parts. Since individual prices are given in the captions, the prices of component parts of the sets will not be listed again.

We hope that some of the information that we have assembled will be of interest to you whether it is something you intend to collect of not. Just knowing a little more about Imperial Glass Corporation should add to everyone's enjoyment.

Credits

Quoted material is from Imperial Glass Company booklets, catalogs, and factory papers. The authors are unknown. Glass Collectors are appreciative of all such notes handed down through the years.

Chapter 1
Short History of the Imperial Glass Company

"Pride of workmanship, skill, and a deep devotion to quality were the prime motivators of Imperial's glassworkers."

A group of investors organized the Imperial Glass Company in 1901. After a period of "several years of construction, installing furnaces, and creating a number of initial moulds," the first Imperial glass was produced in 1904 in Bellaire, Ohio.

Imperial's earliest production was clear pressed glass. Sales were made to the five and dime stores for items such as covered butter dishes, berry bowls and pickle dishes. These lines expanded into lampshades, jelly glasses, pitchers, salt and pepper shakers, sugars and creamers, and other similar types of glass.

The period of 1910 to 1929 saw several new Imperial lines. In this group were the colored and frosted electric lamp shades in an imitation "Tiffany" style. First line was Nuart iridescent ware. Following Nuart, Imperial introduced Nucut Crystal, which was a hand-pressed reproduction of English cut glass. "Collectors Crystal" was a reintroduction (1950s) of the Nucut line and was one of Imperial's most popular giftware lines.

"Imperial Jewels . . . exquisite freehand iridescent 'stretch glass' items" were introduced in 1916. This was a "high point" of Imperial's production that involved many shops making pressed wares as well as blown and freehand ware.

From 1904 to 1922 the company flourished, though the market changed as machine made glassware came to the forefront. In 1922, the mass-produced glass markets caused Imperial to try new ideas, including the creation of Imperial's "Art Glass," an innovation that proved to be unsuccessful.

In 1929 the forces of the Depression, combined with further loss of major markets, forced Imperial to enter bankruptcy. The company continued operations while under the direction of receivership. With an order from Quaker Oats Company in 1931 for a premium to be packaged in its product, Imperial was able to stay in business. The company reorganized under the name Imperial Glass Corporation.

The Quaker Oats premium was the "forerunner of today's Cape Cod pattern," a line that survived until the demise of Imperial in 1984. Another jewel to continue until the closing in 1984 was Candlewick, a pattern that was introduced in 1936. Candlewick contained the largest number of items in any Imperial line. It eventually became more popular than the earlier favorite, Cape Cod.

A 1930s catalog pictured thirty pieces of opal glass in this period. According to the only 1930s price list available, Imperial produced twenty-four pieces of opal glass in 1932. These are the earliest company documentations found on milk glass produced by Imperial Glass Company. The height of milk glass production of approximately six hundred items was in the 1950s, with production falling off to less than forty items made after 1970. February 1, 1951, was the introduction of the famous IG hallmark that was in use for twenty-three years. This mark is often found on Imperial milk glass items.

Imperial had many private mould customers. Companies and individuals brought their moulds to Imperial for glass items to be specially made. Imperial also supplied items from its own lines to many different distributors and private mould customers that then added decorations and marketed these items under their company's name. A few of those companies were Sear Roebuck Inc., Butler Brothers, Lightolier [Lighting] Company, Keystone Silver, Inc. Midwest Chandelier Company, and Irving W. Rice, Inc.

At the beginning of World War II, changes began taking shape in imports. American companies could no longer import glass products from European countries. Irving W. Rice, NY, was a major importer of colognes and powder boxes. With the onset of the war, Irving W. Rice (AKA Irice) turned to Imperial Glass Corporation to supply the dresser items for which Irice was so well known. The year 1939 was the beginning of a long, strong relationship between the two companies that continued through the 1940s. Correspondence in the late 1960s suggested that the two companies were attempting to resume relations. However, in 1972 when Lenox bought Imperial Glass Corporation, most private mould work ceased.

Imperial began acquiring glass companies in 1940. First purchased was Central Glass Works (1940), followed by the purchase of the moulds of the Heisey Company (1958). Two lines from the Heisey Company became strong Imperial lines. Heisey Provincial and Old Williamsburg were produced by Imperial in Crystal as well as colors. The purchase of Cambridge Glass Company (1960) added Rosepoint and a strong line of candelabra.

World War II and the postwar period were the boom years of Imperial's production, Not surprisingly, the peak of production of Cape Cod and Candlewick was reached and sustained during this time. Contributing to this were the marriages of young people going to and returning from the war and the strong economy that followed.

In 1972, seeing the need for capital investment, Imperial stockholders arranged a stock exchange with Lenox Incorporated. This was accomplished December 29, 1972, and in 1973, Lenox began marking Imperial glass with "LIG". In June 1981, Arthur Lorch, a private investor, purchased the company from Lenox. The new mark, "ALIG", began appearing in 1982 and was used only during that year. In the fall of 1982, Lenox foreclosed on its note with Mr. Lorch.

Robert F. Stahl, Jr., a management consultant, bought the company in late 1982, and filed for Chapter 11 bankruptcy in an effort to reorganize the company. A small amount of glass produced carried the NI mark for "New Imperial". The last day of general production was June 15, 1984. Appropriately, the last item off the production line was a four-inch swan with 6-15-84, in raised numbers on the inside. In August 1984 after all efforts failed, liquidation was ordered. Consolidated Liquidation Company and Lancaster Colony combined to purchase the assets of Imperial Glass Corporation and proceeded to sell the last remnants of the bankrupt business. Liquidation was completed with the sale of the building to Mrs. Anna Maroon in March 1985.

Mrs. Maroon invested much time and money trying to find a business to occupy the defunct Imperial factory building. It was her desire to provide an economic stimulus to Bellaire, Ohio and, at the same time, preserve the historical building that meant much to so many people for many years. The anchor of this endeavor was the Imperial Hayshed. Originally, the Hayshed had been the storage place for hay used in packing glass to be shipped. During the later years, the Hayshed was an outlet for research and development pieces and factory seconds. From 1985 to 1995, the Hayshed was an Imperial glass consignment shop that was often the first stop for collectors attending the annual convention of the National Imperial Glass Collectors' Society.

The Bellaire Glass and Artifacts Museum played a vital part in drawing visitors to the partially renovated factory building. There were other tenants, but not enough to fulfill the dream of saving the Imperial Glass Corporation factory building. The building was razed in June 1995. The Hayshed outlet was moved to a building on adjacent property. After a few years, the Hayshed was closed. Standing on the ground where the Imperial Glass Corporation once stood is now a shopping center. A black top parking lot covers the area where collectors once spent hours and days searching for shards, and reminiscing about the greatness of Imperial Glass.

The following marks are those used by Imperial to mark its wares. These are the dates the marks were actually registered, or are generally accepted as used for the first time. We do not have registration records for Nuart, but it preceded the Nucut mark.

Imperial's Marks

Imperial Glass Company existed from 1901 to 1931. After reorganizing in 1931, Imperial Glass Corporation operated until 1984.

In 2003, after many years of talking, dreaming, and planning, the National Imperial Glass Collectors' Society opened the National Imperial Museum. It is now possible for collectors to take a walk back in time and view examples of the wonderful glass that Imperial produced for the enjoyment of generations past, present, and future.

We wrote in our first book, *Imperial Cape Cod Tradition to Treasure,* ©1982, " . . . as collectors of Imperial Glass, we have a strong feeling that Imperial will never lose it identity as a producer of fine crystal. In a mass production world, 'Imperial continues to create only handcrafted glassware. Pride of workmanship, skill, and a deep devotion to quality are the prime motivators of Imperial's glassworkers.'" With the close of Imperial, this should be restated: "Imperial continued to create only handcrafted glassware. Pride of workmanship, skill, and a deep devotion to quality were the prime motivators of Imperial's glassworkers." (Quoted parts of this history have been condensed from *A Consumer and Retail Guide to Handcrafted Glassware*, Imperial Glass Corp., Bellaire, OH 43906. Remaining information was obtained through printed information from old records of the Imperial Glass Corporation.)

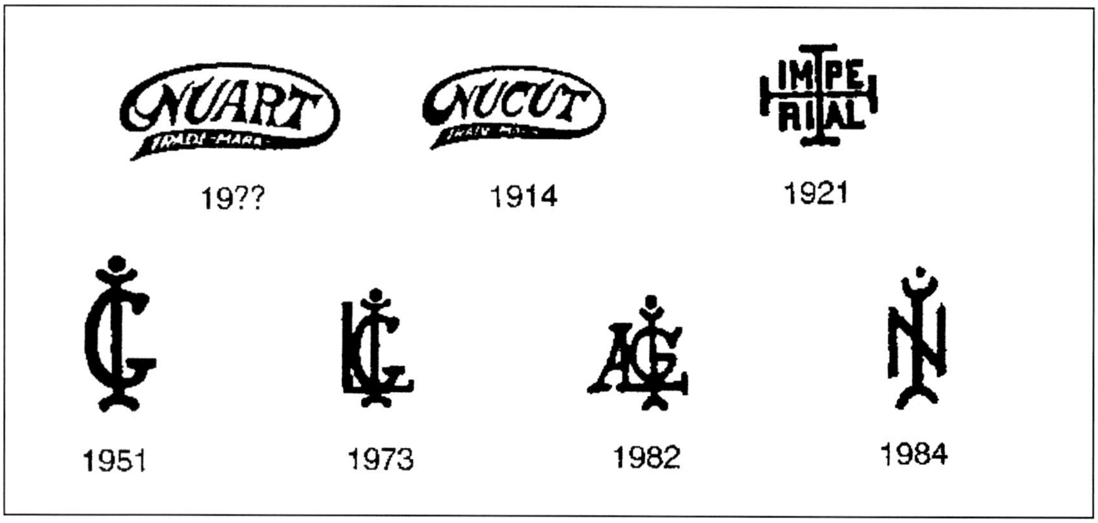

Chapter 2
Patterns

It is difficult to find a single approach to convey information about some of the patterns and colors for a company with as large a production as that of Imperial Glass Company. In an attempt to share with collectors a small portion of Imperial's lines, three approaches will be used; patterns, colors, and categories.

Almost every pattern and every item in this book has one or more possible locations. Items we first placed in the special sections seemed to be more appropriate in a pattern group. Other times an item in a color group needed to be in the pattern group. There were instances when an item found its way back to the original placement. It made the placement look like musical chairs.

In some instances, Imperial sold an item from the general line to a distributor or decorator known as a Private Mould Customer. If a regular production item in a pattern was also sold to a Private Mould Customer that item will be illustrated in a pattern section. The final placement decision reached was that, as nearly as possible, *illustrated* items would be grouped in the pattern group rather than in the Private Mould Customer information.

"Zippered Heart," #292: made 1906-1920, again in 1940 and the 1960s

Imperial's pattern #292, AKA, "Zippered Heart," began in 1906 and consisted of twenty-one items. The line was phased out about 1920. The pattern did not include ordinary pieces such as plates, cups, and saucers or other place settings; it consisted of punch set, pitcher and tumblers, covered butter, sherbet, sugar and creamer, bowls, vases and nappies. Although approximately twenty pieces are in shown in catalogs, we do know of over forty items; there can easily be more that we do not know about.

The general pattern number #292 identified the pieces. Occasionally the number will vary slightly to designate the type of item. For the pieces in the photographs that we have not identified by catalog illustration, the general number #292 will be in parenthesis.

Irving W. Rice, AKA Irice, was an American distributor of dresser accessories from 1904 until the present time as this company is still in business. When World War II made it impossible to import products, Irice started buying domestic goods. Imperial was one of its main sources of glass dresser items and other tabletop pieces. You will find more Irice information in the Private Mould Customers Section.

In the late 1930s, an advertisement illustrated the Zippered Heart dresser set named "The Duchess." It was described as being designed by Czechoslovakian artisans in an American factory. This ad refers to the set made in the Imperial factory. Naturally, some collectors today mistakenly refer to it being a Czechoslovakian set. The following photographs of the Zipper Heart set are examples of items sold in the late 1930s into the 1940s to Irving W. Rice.

A spectacular piece of Zippered Heart was bought just before the passed deadline for this book. It is the #2929C without the usual crimped shape. The measurements are 12" diameter and 7" height. The glass is sparkling clear. A photograph would not have done it justice.

#292 Punch Bowl Set, 10" Bowl; 12 Cups, 5 oz. $220-250.

#292, 5 oz. Custard, AKA Punch Cup. $15-18.

#2929C, 12" Orange Bowl, 6 1/2" deep. $85-95.

(#292), 12" Orange Bowl, 7 1/2" deep. Noted on company catalog page, this item was made in Rose Pink (color #64) for special orders only. $100-110.

#292E, 8" Banana Bowl, 13 1/2" width. $65-75.

(#292), 9 1/2" Bowl, footed, 7" tall (two sides higher). $75-95.

(#292), 11" Crimped Bowl, footed, 6" tall. $65-75.

(#292), 10" Crimped Bowl, 8" tall. $65-75.

(#292), 9" Vase, footed, 6 1/2" top. $75-85.

(#292), 14" Bowl, 5 1/2" tall. $110-125.

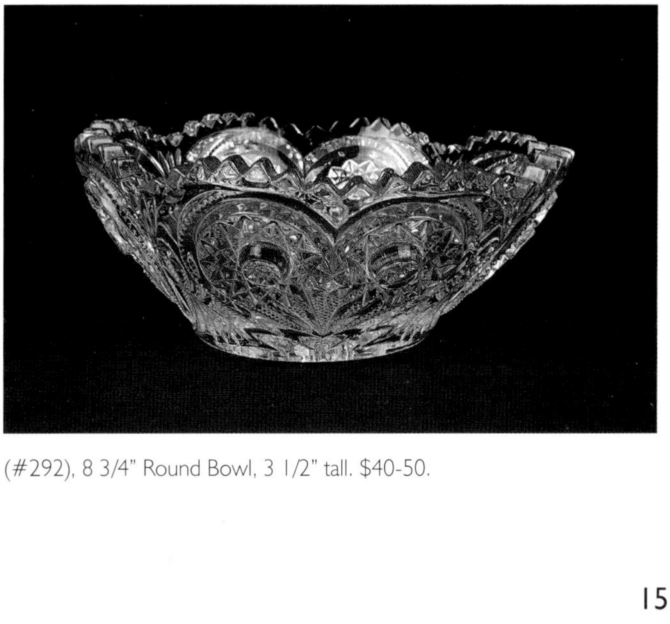

(#292), 8 3/4" Round Bowl, 3 1/2" tall. $40-50.

(292), 9 1/2" Round Bowl, 2 3/4" deep. $35-45.

(#292), 9" Crimped Bowl, 3 3/4" deep. $35-45.

(#292), 10" Shallow Crimped Bowl, 2 3/4" deep. $35-45.

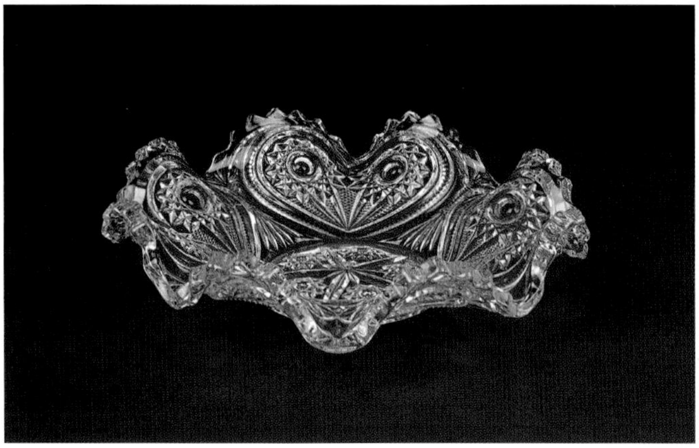

(#292), 10" Round Crimped Bowl, 2 1/2" tall. $35-45.

#2922A, 4 1/4" Jelly, 4 1/2" tall. $25-35.

#2922A, 4 1/4" Jelly, 4 1/2" tall; #2921A, 4" Sherbet, 4" tall. $25-35.

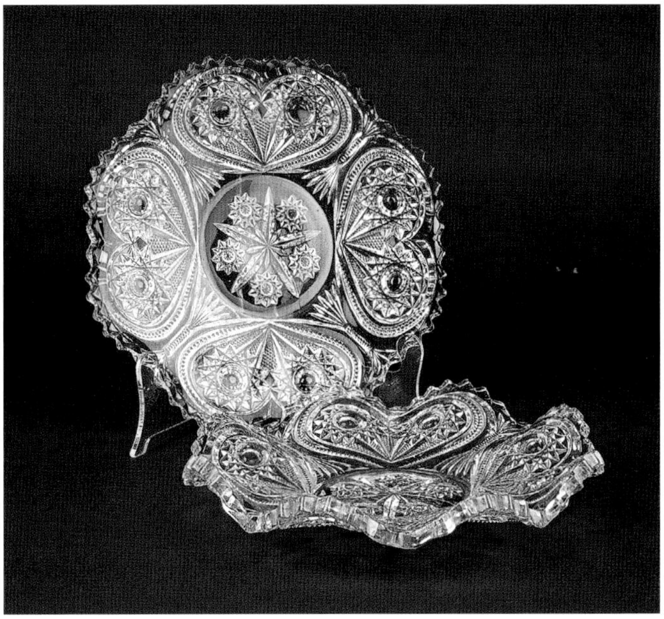

(#292), 10 1/2" Flat Plate, back; 10" Crimped Plate, front. $35-45.

#2922N, 3 1/2" Rose Bowl, 4 1/2" tall; #2921N, 3 1/2" Rose Bowl, 4" tall (note plain edge). $45-55.

#2925A, 4" Round Vase, round, 5" tall, (two examples with slight difference at top edge). $35-45.

#2925E, 6" Fan Vase, 5" tall. $65-75.

#2925B, 4 1/2" Vase, (cone shape). $50-55; (#292), 8" Vase, (cone shape) $85-95. We did not know the larger version existed until recently. It is the same shape as the 4 1/2" Vase, Cone.

#292, 7", Sugar and Cover. $55-60.

#292, Open Cream, open top has the pointed edge. $25-30.

#2927S, 4" Individual Sugar, square, (The points are pulled to place the heart on the flat side). $20-22; 2927S, 4" Individual Cream, square, (does not include handles). $20-22.

#2927A, 3 1/2" Round Individual Sugar. $20-22; #2927A, 3 1/2" Round Individual Cream, (does not include handles), #20-22.

#292, 7 1/2" Butter, Covered, base is flat, handled. Base has a small floweret like the one on the foot of the cologne bottle. Base does not have the pattern design of the Zippered Heart. $95-115.

(#292), 8" Butter, Covered; base has the Zippered Heart pattern pressed in it. $85-95.

(#292), 4", Square 2-handled Nappy, (This item has the square points pulled to the center of the heart design; does not include handles). $22-25.

(#292), Mayo Set, a second view of the previous photograph. $45-48.

(#292), 5", 2-Handled Nappy, round, (does not include handles). $22-25.

(#292), 4 1/2" Mayo Bowl, 6" Plate. $45-48 set.

#2927E, 6" Handled Spoon Tray, (does not include handles). $50-55.

(#292), 7" Heart Nappy, (includes handle). $30-35.

(#292), 6" Round Nappy, (does not include handle). $25-28.

#292, 6" Small Pitcher, (including lip) left. $60-65; 8 12" tall Pitcher, on right, (including lip) $65-85.

#292, 4" Tumbler, (catalog illustration). $*

(#292), 3 1/2" Candleholder Cup, (not including handle). This Candleholder was reissued in a group named Collectors Crystal in 1964 through 1967. It was also promoted with a shade as a Handled Candle Lamp. If it is made for the Collectors Crystal group, it could be marked. Items made after 1951 should be marked with the superimposed IG. However, we have not found one with the IG mark. $60-65.

(292), 8" Bowl, slightly turned in at top. $60-65.

(#292), 5" Berry Bowl, Amethyst Carnival, (Mulberry base glass with an iridescent spray applied and fired.) $55-65.

#920 Dresser Set, 10" Cologne Bottle and Stopper, $85-95; #R-921, 4 1/2" Jar and Cover, $50-60; #R-792 19" Tray, $85-95; 1941-1946 made for Irving W. Rice. Reproductions of the bottle and stopper have appeared in the market place. They are visibly inferior and smaller, 8 1/2" tall rather than the 10" tall of Imperial's cologne bottle.

#R-920, 4 1/2" Powder Box, Pink. $100-125.

#R-920, 4 1/2" Powder Box, Pink. A second view.

#R-921, 10" Cologne, Pink. $100-125.

#R-921, 10" Cologne, Blue. $100-125.

#292, 3 1/4" Candleholder, (not including handle); with shade, it is two piece Handled Candle Lamp for Star Exclusive, New Orleans, 1977, Ruby (Amberina [Ruby] in this promotion.) $*.

#292, 3 1/4" Candleholder (not including handle). Although Imperial made some items in Nut Brown for Star Exclusive, this Zippered Heart candleholder is not on the list of items made in Nut Brown for this company. $*.

Reededed, #701: 1930s-1960s

Estimated dates of the various Reeded colors are as follows:

Crystal- late 1930s to 1960s

Stiegel Green #3, Black #4, Hock Green #5, Ritz Blue #6, Ruby #10, Amber #40, Venetian Blue #80- 1930s-1940s

Mustard, Turquoise, Bead Green- 1958

Milk Glass- 1956-1958

Midas- 1958-1960

Since Imperial often called its patterns by numbers only, you will sometimes hear and see Reeded referred to as #701. Imperial's Reeded pattern is one of the little-known patterns of Imperial Glass Company that is gaining the interest of glass collectors. The Spoon and Fork are the most well known pieces in this pattern because they were combined with several of Imperial's other patterns. The Muddler, too, was combined with Old Fashion glasses in other Imperial patterns. Then along came the perfumes and powder boxes that were added to boudoir production and you have another exposure to the Reeded pattern. Reeded is difficult to find because there has not been much collecting activity and therefore many dealers do not buy and offer Reeded for sale.

In early depression glass research, Reeded was given the generic name, "Spun." The name was evidently associated with the design. "Threading" was another misnomer for Imperial's Reeded.

Please keep in mind that Imperial always used the name Ruby; this color was never referred to as red (well, almost never). In researching for this book, we thought we might uncover just one time that the word red was used, but it was always Ruby. All Imperial collectors who have attended the National Imperial Glass Collectors' Society Conventions have learned the lesson of the color name Ruby [never Red] from a devoted teacher of Imperial Glass. We will not name that person, but we collectors know the name well. This lesson is so ingrained in the authors that there are no longer any RED automobiles; they are all RUBY. HOWEVER, there was found one tiny mention of Red, which will be noted later.

Imperial often labeled an item one name in a catalog and then in a later catalog, changed the name slightly. In our books, we use the most often referenced name. We will identify photographed items by color name as much as possible. Since we have a limited number of company color photographs, we sometimes have to decide the color name by the date an item is introduced or by some other small clue, we might find in our research. We hope that we do not confuse any collector with color identification. The greens have proven to be a challenge.

As early as 1937, Butler Brothers, Chicago, Illinois, a mail order catalog company, ordered twelve pieces of the Reeded pattern in Crystal, Amber, and Hock Green. That information will be listed in the Private Mould Section.

In addition to the early catalog, we have a 1937 price list that listed over thirty items. Listed below are the Reeded items that can be found in Hock Green, Ruby, Ritz Blue, Amber, Venetian Blue and Crystal during the late 1930s.

#701, 80 oz. Jug
#701, 12 oz. Ice Tea
#701, 5 oz. Juice
#701, Bitters and Tube
#701 7 oz. Old Fashion Cocktail
#701, 12 oz. Hiball
#701, 3 1/2 oz. Cocktail
#7012, 3 1/2 oz. Cocktail
#701, Shaker and Top
#701, Muddler
#701, Ice Tub
#701/1, 5" Rose Bowl
#701/2, 6" Rose Bowl
#701/3, 5" Bud vase
#701/4, 9" Vase
#701/5, 2 1/2" Ball
#701/6, 4" Ball
#701/7, 6" Ball, Crystal Foot
#701/8, Candleholder, Crystal Foot
#701/9, 2 1/2" Ball, Crystal Foot
#701/10, 4" Ball, Crystal Foot
#7014F, 4 1/2" Fruit
#7016W, 7" Nappy
#7018B, 10" Bowl
#7018D, 14" Plate
#7018V, 13 1/2" Plate
#7016D, 8" Plate
#701, Cup and Saucer
#701, Sugar and Cream
#701, 2-pc. Smoker
#701, 2 1/2" Cigarette Holder
#701, 2" Ash Tray
#701, Candleholder and Insert
#701, 3-pc. Mayonnaise
#701, Candy Jar and Cover
#701, 10 oz. Water

#701: Crystal: 1930s to 1960s

#701, 2 1/2" Candleholder, Crystal. $25-30. Note the removable insert; it is best described as a large thimble. This insert could easily be separated from its holder at an estate or similar sale. On the right is the #701/2, 6" Rose Bowl, Crystal. $20-25.

#701, 2 1/2" Candleholder; another look at the insert for the Candleholder, Crystal.

#701, 4 1/4" Candleholder, round, Crystal. $20-22.

#701/1, 5" Vase. In our early research for this book, this vase presented a puzzle; it did not have the same number of crimps as the Turquoise cased over milk glass shown on page 47. When a picture of the Midas Vase was found on 1957 catalog pages, it was exciting to see the top opening had the same number of crimps (8) as the Crystal vase. This Crystal vase is the same shape as the Midas, but it does not have the gold paint applied. If several more of the Crystal ones are found, it will probably determine that it is a regular production item, otherwise it was intended to be the Midas production item, but was not decorated. $25-35.

#7012, 12 oz. Tumbler. $10-12; #701, 5 oz. Juice. $10-12; #701, 7 oz. Old Fashioned, Crystal. $12-15, (note the slanted, rather than straight sides on Old Fashioned.)

#701, 3 1/2 oz. Cocktail, Crystal. $12-15.

#70181B, 10" Bowl, snap bottom, Crystal. $25-35.

#70181B, 10" Bowl, snap bottom. (defined in opening of book), Crystal. $30-35.

#701, Cup and Saucer, Crystal. $15-20.

#701/4, 9" Vase, (concave), Crystal. $35-40.

#701B, 11 1/2" Tall Boy Shaker with Bamboo wrapped handle. In the 1930s, there was a 36 oz. 9 1/2" Shaker in Crystal, Ruby, Ritz Blue and Amber; these will be shown in the appropriate color sections, unknown distributor. $*.

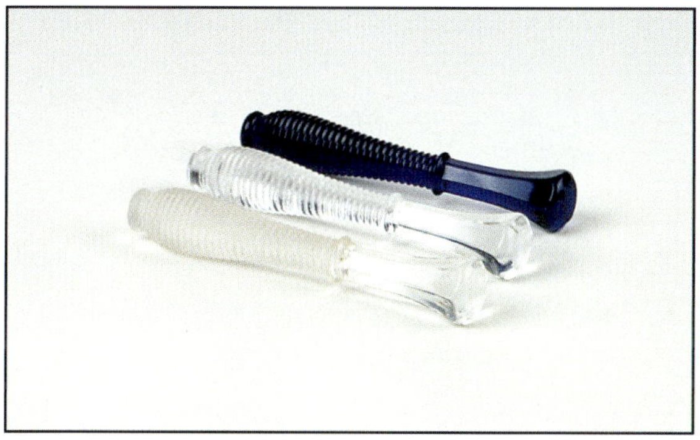

#701, Muddler, Crystal Satin, Crystal. $10-12; Ritz Blue. $22-25. Late acquisitions of Amber and Stiegel Green will be shown in later sections.

#701, 3 oz. Bitters Bottle, Crystal. $30-40.

#701, 10 1/2", 26 oz. Dunce Cap Decanter, with #701, 3 oz. Whiskey Tumbler Top. $40-50; #701, 9 1/2", 18 oz. Dunce Cap Decanter, with #701, 5 oz., Juice Tumbler Top. $45-50.

"Colossus" is an understatement for this next item. Can you believe a Cocktail Shaker that stands 18" tall and holds 80 oz.? It takes both hands to hold it and pour. In fact, you might need a friend to help pour from this shaker. It comes in Crystal only and with the addition of eight, 7 1/2 oz. Whiskey Sour glasses, it is the #7019, 9 pc. Cocktail Set. This Colossus Shaker was cataloged from 1958 to 1961. We were fortunate that a friend spotted this shaker in a mall and gave us a call. We have only seen this one.

#701, 80 oz. Colossus Shaker, Crystal.

During this same time (1958-1961,) there was a 48 oz. Cocktail Shaker, 11 1/4" tall, produced in Crystal, Turquoise, Mustard, and Bead Green. Examples of the color shakers will be shown with appropriate color group.

As mentioned previously, the Spoon and Fork set was sold separately and was offered with several different Imperial patterns, e.g. Candlewick, Cape Cod, Washington, Pillar Flute, Empire, and others. The Spoon and Fork can be found in Crystal, Viennese Blue, Yellow, Green, and Black. In addition to the easy to find Crystal, there is an elusive set called "White, Frosted by acid dipping." The handles are frosted and the rest is clear. Collectors would likely call the set "Crystal Frosted" or "Satin Crystal."

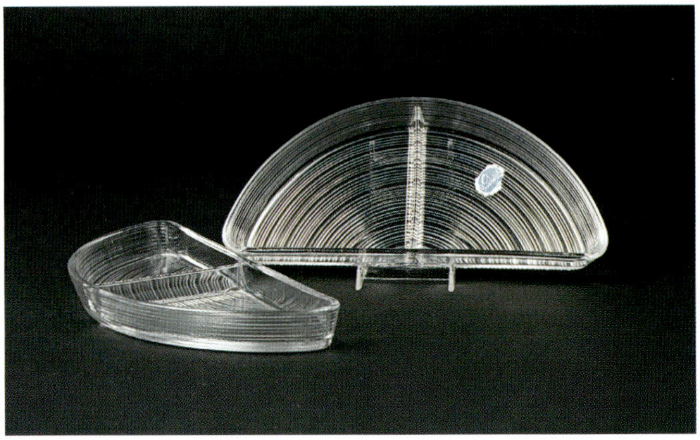

#701, 9 1/4" Relish End, Crystal. According to an Imperial memorandum in 1948, this item was sold to Superior Electric Products Corporation. It is difficult to imagine how this piece might be used in an electrical product. $35-45.

#701, Perfume with Atomizer, made using the Bitters Bottle, Crystal. The fit of the atomizer seems to make this item an original. Note the cork part of the atomizer inside the neck. $25-35.

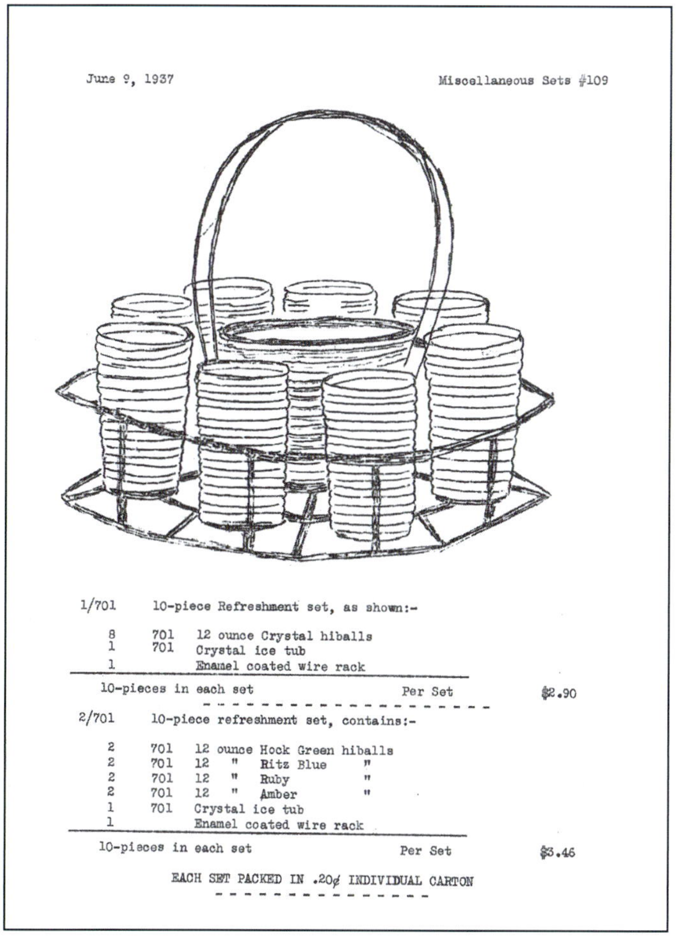

June 9, 1937 Miscellaneous Sets #109

1/701	10-piece Refreshment set, as shown:-		
8	701	12 ounce Crystal hiballs	
1	701	Crystal ice tub	
1		Enamel coated wire rack	
	10-pieces in each set	Per Set	$2.90
2/701	10-piece refreshment set, contains:-		
2	701	12 ounce Hock Green hiballs	
2	701	12 " Ritz Blue "	
2	701	12 " Ruby "	
2	701	12 " Amber "	
1	701	Crystal ice tub	
1		Enamel coated wire rack	
	10-pieces in each set	Per Set	$3.46

EACH SET PACKED IN .20¢ INDIVIDUAL CARTON

Company sketch, 1937, A 10 pc. Refreshment Set, Enameled Coated Wire Pack held eight 12 oz. Hiball tumblers in color with a Crystal Ice Tub. Available tumbler colors were Ritz Blue, Hock Green, Ruby, and Amber. The 12 oz. Tumbler in a previous photograph on page 26 would be in this set.

This 8 crimped rose bowl is undocumented in Crystal. It would be the Midas Bowl if it had the gold applied. If more in Crystal are found, it might be a production item. $25-35

Reeded #701 Ruby: 1930s

#701/10, 4" Ball, Crystal Foot. $35-45; #701/7, 6" Ball, Crystal Foot, Ruby. $40-50. The Crystal Foot was sometimes referred to as a "cast foot."

#701/10, 4" Ball, Crystal Foot. $35-45; #701/6, 4" Rose Bowl, Ruby. $35-40.

#701/8, 2 1/2" Candleholder, Crystal Foot, Ruby. The candle insert resembles a large thimble. $35-40.

#701, 4" Ball Smoker, Ruby. Insert for the 2-pc. Ball Smoker is a "V" shape glass part and has three resting places for cigarettes. $75-90.

#701/4, 9" Vase, Ruby. $55-65.

#701/3, 5" Bud Vase, Ruby. $25-35.

#701, 5" Mayo, 5 1/4" Under Plate, Ruby. $35-40 set.

#7016W, 7" Nappy, Ruby. $15-20.

#701, 3 1/2 oz. Cocktail. $18-20; #7012, 3 1/2 oz. Cocktail, Crystal Foot. $20-22; top, #701, 7 oz. Old Fashion, Ruby. $20-25.

On a 1938 factory price list, we found a reference to an interesting item, a 3-pc. Coffee Serving Set, #6/701. It consisted of a Crystal Coffee Jug with a wooden handle and Ruby stopper. The rest of the set is a Ruby Coaster or Tile for the jug to rest on. To complete the set, it is combined with a cup and saucer. Imperial occasionally did not count a stopper or some other part of a group of items. It was also produced in Ritz Blue. When a fellow collector shared his find of this jug, we were able to share with him the paper documentation.

#701, 8" Trivet, Ruby; $40-45. There are three small oblong feet on the underside of the trivet. This Trivet is part of the 10/#701, 3-pc. Coffee Serving Set. $*.

Reeded #701, Ritz Blue: circa late 1930s

Please refer to the Ruby section for information on the 3-pc. Coffee Serving Set that can also be found with Ritz Blue glass parts.

Not shown in any catalogs that we have is an interesting pitcher that has now been found in Ritz Blue. Two collectors found this pitcher and sent photographs for identification. Fortunately, we were able to identify it from a simple company sketch. In company records, we found a memorandum to the sales representatives, detailing, "the #7011 Ball Pitcher is now changed to a #7012 Tall Pitcher, and the #7011 Concave Tumbler is changed to a new straight-sided Hiball #7012." That memorandum with basic sketches of the two new items helped us to verify that the collectors' find was a production item.

#701, 80 oz. Pitcher with ice lip, Ritz Blue. $ $75-80.

#701, 7 pc. Ice Tea or Beverage Set; #701, 80 oz. Pitcher. $75-80; #701, 12 oz. Tumblers, Ritz Blue. $15-20.

(#701), Tumbler, 12 oz.; (#701) Tumbler, Small, 5 oz., Ritz Blue. $ Note the protruding ridge at the base of each tumbler. It is similar to the base ridge on the #701, 3 1/2" Cocktail, except between the tumbler and the foot is a 1/4" straight separation that has three "reeds" on it. We cannot find a catalog picture or reference of this item. $35-50 each.

#701, 3 1/2 oz. Cocktail, Ritz Blue. $20-22.

#7014F, 4 1/2" Fruit, Ritz Blue. $15-18.

#7018B, 10" Bowl, deep, Ritz Blue. $50-60; #701, Reeded Spoon and Fork, Crystal. $20-22.

#701/1, 5" Rose Bowl, Ritz Blue. $40-50.

#701/2, 6" Rose Bowl, Ritz Blue. $35-40; #701/5, 2 1/2" Ball, Ritz Blue. $25-30

#701/7, 6" Rose Bowl, Crystal Foot, Ritz Blue. $45-55.

#701, 2-pc., 4" Ball Smoker, Ritz Blue, the insert for the Ball Smoker is "V" shape and has three resting places for cigarettes. The base of the V insert is open to allow ashes to fall through into the ball. $85-100.

#701/6, 4" Rose Bowl, Ritz Blue. $17-20.

#701/3, 5" Bud Vase, Wrought Iron Holder, Ritz Blue. $39-40; #701/3, 5" Bud Vase, Ritz Blue. $20-25.

#701/5, 2 1/2" Ball, Wrought Iron Holder, Ritz Blue. $30-40.

#701, Syrup, Servit; 4" Ball, Ritz Blue, (Servit in raised letters, on top of the metal handle); this item probably was made for a special order, but we have no paper documentation. $90-95.

We think that the following photograph may be the referenced Hiball. This tumbler does not match any other reference that we have so it is a possibility that it is the one in the sketch.

#701, 36 oz. Shaker, Chrome Plated top; Ritz Blue $95-100; #701, 3 1/2 oz. Cocktail, Ritz Blue $20-22; This shaker with the early version top is one of the most difficult to find.

#7012, Tall Pitcher, Ritz Blue. $*. #7012, 12 oz. Hiball. $40-50.

Reeded #701, Stiegel Green: late 1930s

Stiegel is a beautiful Emerald Green. Imperial used it in many of its lines through these early years.

#701, 4" Ball Smoker; Ash Tray. Note the insert shown at the left of the photograph. Stiegel Green. $100-125 set.

#701, 4" Ball Smoker; Cigarette Holder, and Ash Tray, Stiegel Green. $100-125 set

#7011, 80 oz. Ice Tea Pitcher. $70-80; #701, Ice 12 oz. Tea Tumbler, Stiegel Green. $18-20.

#701, 6" Bud Vase, Forester, Stiegel Green. $35-40.

#701, Creamer, Stiegel Green. $15-17.

#701, Cup and Saucer, Stiegel Green. $20-22.

#701, 7 oz. Old Fashion Tumbler, Stiegel Green. $18-20; #701, 3 1/2 oz. Cocktail, Stiegel Green. $15-18.

#701/3, 5" Bud Vase, Wrought Iron holder, Stiegel Green. We believe that the top of these vases were altered after leaving the factory. Originally, the tops would have been crimped. In addition, they are a little shorter. There is a possibility they were not crimped and therefore they were not stretched to the full height. We are only including this example for collectors to see another color in the wrought iron. Not Priced.

#701, Old Fashion Tumbler, $18-20; 36 oz. Shaker, Stiegel Green. $85-95.

Reedeed #701, Hock Green: 1930s

This is a little-known color name; it is only with company price lists, and listing items produced in this color that we could determine the group of examples that are shown here. The key to find that determination was a company note that the #7018f Bowl was made with a snap (marie) bottom. That set listed in factory paper as being made in Hock Green is the only set in the Reeded group with a snap bottom that we have found.

#701, Decanter, (missing shot glass top), Hock Green, if complete. $55-60.

#701, 12 oz. Ice Tea, Hock Green. $12-14.

#7018V, 13 1/2" Plate, cupped, Hock Green. $30-35; #701B, 10" Bowl; both plates have ground bottoms, Hock Green. $30-35.

#7018D, 14" Plate, flat, ground bottom, Hock Green. $30-35; #7018B, 10 Bowl, snap bottom, Hock Green. $30-35.

#701/9, 3" Ball, Crystal Foot, Hock Green. $20-25.

#701, 5" Mayo. $10-12; #701, Under Plate, snap bottom, Hock Green. $10-12.

#701, 9" Vase, Hock Green. $45-55.

#701, Creamer, Hock Green. $10-12.

#701, 3 1/2 oz. Cocktail, Hock Green, Crystal Foot. $12-15.

Reeded, #701, "Early" Amber: late 1930s

The early Amber Reeded pieces had a slightly rosier tint than the Amber introduced in the early 1940s. The later Amber color was a darker and more dense color.

Reeded #701, "Late" Amber: 1940s

Listed on a 1955 company papers were three #701, Forrester Vases measuring 6", 8", and 10". The colors initially were Crystal, Turquoise, Stiegel Green, and Mustard; Madeira and Bead Green were added later.

#701, Ice Tea or Beverage Set; #701, 80 oz. Ice Lip Pitcher. $50-60; #701, 12 oz. Ice Tea, Amber. $15-18.

#701, 80 oz. Pitcher, Amber. $50-60.

#701, Sugar. $10-12; #701, 3 1/2 oz. Cocktail, Amber. $12-15.

#70181D, 14" Plate, back. $30-35; #7016D, 8" Plate, Salad, front, Amber. $30-35.

#701/2, 6" Rose Bowl, Amber. $30-35.

#701/7, 6" Ball, Rose Bowl, Crystal Foot, Amber. $35-45.

#701/8, 2 1/2" Candleholder, Crystal Foot, Amber. $20-25.

#701, 9 1/2" Fork and Spoon Set, Amber, Set. $30-40.

#701/3, 5" Bud Vase, Wrought Iron holder, Amber. $20-22.

#701, 3 1/2 oz. Cocktail, Amber. $15-18; #7018V, 13 1/2" Plate, cupped, Amber. $30-35; #7011, 80 oz. Pitcher, Crystal with Amber Handle. $75-85.

#701, Muddler, Amber, Stiegel Green, Crystal. $18-22.

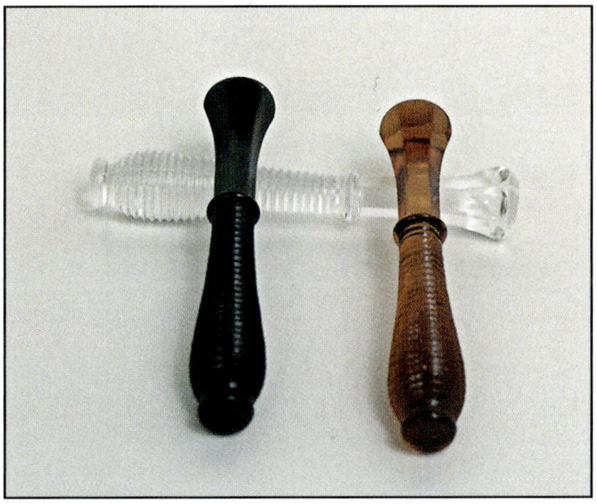

Another listing in 1955-56 was the #701, "Dunce Cap" Decanter that was made in two sizes. An 18 oz. (9 1/2") was combined with the #701, 5 oz. Juice for the top. The 26 oz. (10 1/2") Decanter was combined with #701, 3 oz., Whiskey Tumbler Top. The Dunce Cap Decanter was made in Smoke, Turquoise, Mustard, Bead Green, and Crystal.

Also in 1955, the Reeded Shaker, called "Tall Boy," 48 ounces, 11 1/4", was made in several colors, and combined with tops of chrome or bronze, e.g.; Smoke/chrome, Black/chrome, Stiegel Green/bronze, Crystal/bronze. In 1956, the Tall Boy was also made in Bead Green, Turquoise, and Madera. This time the letter "B" indicated the Bronze or Brass top and the letter "C" was the Chrome top.

Found on a 1956 price list was #701/6, #701/8, and #701/10; for an 8 oz., 16 oz., and 28 oz. Bottle and Stopper, in Turquoise, Bead Green, and Mustard. These are the same as the three bottles and stoppers shown in the Midas group with gold decoration.

Reeded, #701, Smoke

#701, 10 1/2", 26 oz. Dunce Cap Decanter, Smoke. $55-65.

Reeded, #701, Bead Green: 1956

#701, 11 1/4" Shaker, Tall Boy, Bead Green. $45-55.

Reeded, #701, Midas: 1957-1960s

Midas is Crystal with fired on gold. The fourteen cataloged items in the Midas line are as follows:

- #701, Vase, 6"
- #701, Vase, 8"
- #701, Vase, 10"
- #701/6, Bottle and Stopper, 8 oz.
- #701/8, Bottle and Stopper, 16 oz.
- #701/10, Bottle and Stopper, 28 oz.
- #702, Jar and Cover, 5"
- #703, Jar and Cover, 6"
- #704, Jar and Cover, 7"
- #705, Jar and Cover, 8"
- #701, Candy Box and Cover
- #701/1, Rose Bowl, Vase, 5"
- #701/2, Rose Bowl Vase, Round, 6"
- #701/4, Vase, 9"

#701/1, 5" Rose Bowl, Vase, Crimp, Midas. $45-55.

#701/8, 16 oz. Bottle and Stopper, Midas. $65-75. Also made, #701/6, 8 oz.; #701/10, 28 oz.; Midas. $*.

#701/8, 16 oz. Bottle. $65-75; #701, 3 oz. Shot, Midas. $15-20.

#701/4, 9" Vase, Crimped, Midas. $75-85.

#701, 6" and 8" Vase, Midas. $65-70 each.

#701, Candy and Cover, Midas. $45-55.

Reedeed, #701, Pink: 1956-1958

#701/2, 6" Rose Bowl, Vase, Pink $25-30.

#701, 9 3/4" Vase, note Reeded design goes to the top of the opening, Pink, Turquoise. $30-35.

Reeded, #701, Milk Glass: 1950s

#702, 5" and #703, 6" Canister, Milk Glass. $20-25 each.

#701, 11 1/4" Shaker, "Tall Boy," Milk Glass. $40-45.

Reedded, #701, Black: 1955

#701, 11 1/4" Shaker, "Tall Boy", Black. $50-55.

Reeded, #701, Mustard: 1955-1956

#701, 11 1/4" "Tall Boy" Shaker, Mustard. $40-45.

#701, 26 oz. "Dunce Cap" Decanter, Whiskey Tumbler Top, Mustard. $40-45.

Reeded, #701, Viennese Blue AKA Venetian Blue: 1930s

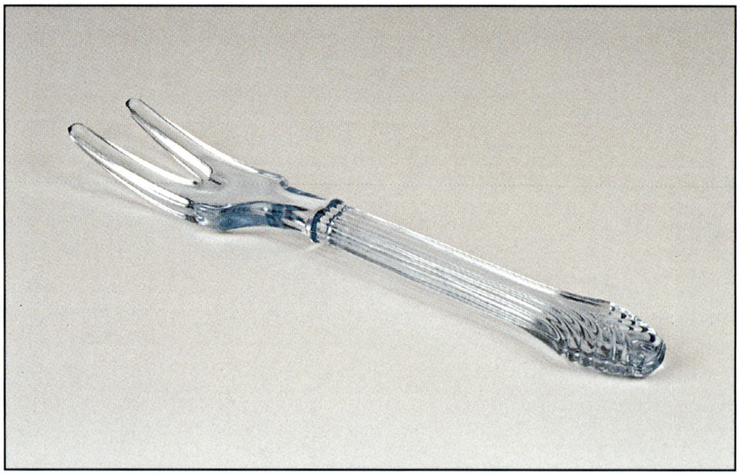

#701, Fork, Viennese Blue. $20-25.

Turquoise, Mustard, Pink, Whirlspool Jars- 1956-1958

#701, Jars, 5", 6" and 8", Pink; 6", 7" Mustard, 6" 7" 8" Turquoise, without knobs. $25-45 each.

#701, Jars, 5", 6" and 8", Pink; 6" 7" Mustard, 6", 7", with knobs. $25-45 each.

Reeded, #701, Cased Over Milk Glass: early 1950s

#701, Vase, Cased Aquamarine over Milk Glass, 6 crimp top. $65-80.

Reeded, #701, Painted and Stained

The 1950s were years that Imperial was strongly promoting the Reeded pattern in several colors and with different names. One example is the group name Whirlspool. The four sizes of Jars and Covers are 5", 6", 7", and 8" with a diameter of 4 1/4". They are available in Turquoise, Pink, Mustard, and Crystal.

The following meager information is included to help collectors with identification if additional documentation is found in the future. On a company paper dated 1956, Imperial offered six Reeded items with an unusual name, Whirled Colors. We think this reference might be for items found with painted interiors. Listed on this 1956 paper are the following pieces:

- 15 oz. Tumbler
- 9 1/2 oz. Tumbler
- 5 oz. Tumbler
- 5 1/2 oz. Sherbet, Footed
- 8" Plate
- Candy Box and Cover

Could the following photographs be examples of the Whirled Colors? We hope so.

There is also another possible answer for these items with the painted insides. In a late 1930s catalog, there is a #1 Flower Pot and Saucer, pressed in three colors; Jade Green, Carmine Red, and Sky Blue. The description said the colors on flowerpot and saucer are put on by hand and highly fired and will not wash off. Therein lays the possibility for the colored items in the previous photographs. These descriptions are mentioned in hope that someone can help solve this question. (This is the only instance in our 30 years researching factory papers that we have found the word "red.")

On a company paper, dated 1956, was a mention of colors for designated magazines. We were once told that color names that were popular in current trends were often used as Imperial color names. Since we have seen the #701, Reeded Candy with a white finish as well as a light lavender or gray inside, we wonder if the grey might be the Gunmetal for the "House and Garden" colors. No mention was found in company material of these names being used in sales literature or production memorandums for Imperial.

For "House and Garden," the colors given were:

- Gunmetal
- Emerald Green
- Terracotta
- Citron
- Turquoise
- White

For "Living," the colors were:

- Barnum Blue
- Victoria Orange
- Gold Rush
- Sandstone
- Parlor Pine
- Gaslight Green

#701, 15 oz. Tumbler, Pink/Red. $10-12.

#701, 5 1/2 oz. Sherbet, footed, Green. $10-12.

#701, 5 1/2 oz. Sherbet, footed, Yellow. $10-12.

#701, Candy Box and Cover, Green; also, Yellow, "Red", We have seen photos of White and Heather painted interiors. $45-55.

To confuse this issue even more, we show a group of tumblers produced in a faint color. We are not able to place them in a color group, and we acknowledge that these might be the pieces that fit the Whirled Colors.

Now that we have given several possibilities for the items with the painted interiors OR the faint tint of the tumblers. Perhaps a collector or fellow researcher can shed light on this group. Collectors can see what a complicated process it can be to determine information concerning identification of the massive products of Imperial Glass Corporation.

#701, Multi-color, 12 oz. Tumblers, unofficial color names, Crystal, Blue Grey, Yellow. Cranberry, Gold, Purple; straight sides. $10-12.

Reedéd Perfumes and Boxes, #1300: 1930-1940

Imperial Glass Company offered several different perfume and puff sets to "decorators and distributors only" in the late 1930s and the 1940s. We have found one reference in a 1938 memorandum for the #1300 Puff Box and Cover in Ritz Blue. In 1943, there is a reference for the #1300 Perfume with Fan Shape stopper and the #1300 with the Intaglio Stopper.

Initially, the 4-Toed Reeded Perfume bottles came with three different stoppers; the Fan Shape stopper (which is often called the arrow stopper), the Satin Rose, and the square Intaglio (Hoffman) stopper. The square stopper with an incised figure of a man blowing bubbles has a tiny butterfly in the corner. The butterfly is the signature of Hoffman, a famous glasscutter from Czechoslovakia. This same design can be found in a much larger stopper and bottle [Factice, imported]. We have no information why the square stopper is found in the American Imperial Reeded perfume. It is possible that Irving W. Rice brought the stoppers to Imperial in 1939, when Irice contracted with Imperial to produce boudoir accessories.

The Reeded Perfume and Puff Box can be found in several colors and combinations. These sets alone make a fun collection. Shown next are several of the different colors and color combinations.

#701, AKA #1301, Puff Box. $25-30; Perfume with Hoffman Stopper, Amber. $30-35.

#701, AKA #1301, Powder Box, Ritz Blue. $35-40.

Shown in this group is the #701, AKA #1300 Perfume. In front is a Ritz Blue Reeded perfume with a Hoffman stopper; second row, has the same Reeded perfume in Light Green, Pink, Teal, and Amber; all have the Hoffman stopper. Back row, is a Black, Medium Green, Milk Glass, Crystal, and Ritz Blue; all have the arrow stopper. $30-45.

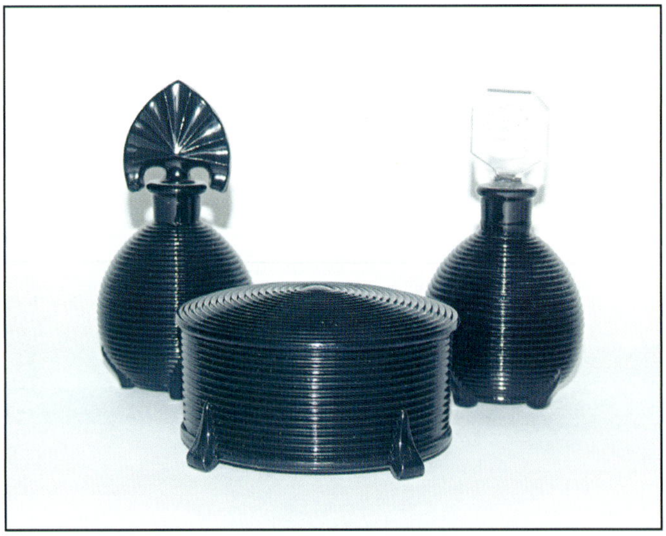

#701, AKA #1300, Perfume, Arrow Stoppers, $35-45; #1301 Puff Box, Black. $35-45.

#701, Perfume AKA #1300, Stiegel Green and Ritz Blue with Arrow Stopper; $30-40; #701 Perfume, Light Green, Pink, Ritz Blue, Hoffman Stoppers. $35-45.

Reeded Lighting Items

It was a struggle deciding whether to put the following lamps and fixtures in the special lighting section or here in the Reeded section. Since it was decided to place them with the pattern group, it seemed appropriate to show them all together rather than in a color group.

Here is another table lamp with Reeded glass parts. At the base is a Reeded Sherbet and above the sherbet are four Reeded balls. This is the original shade, unknown distributor. $55-65.

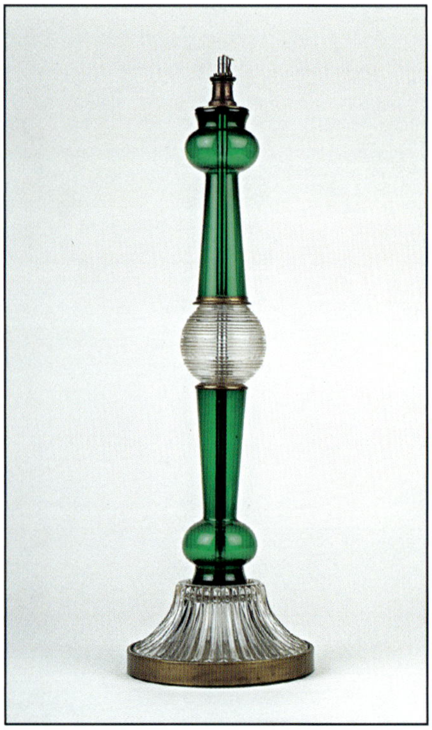

A #701, Reeded Ball added to Hocking Forest Green Vases make up this unusual lamp. It is not known what company bought the Reeded parts from Imperial for this unusual lamp.
You never know where you will find a great addition to your collections. This lamp was found in an open-air flea market, i.e. a cow pasture, in south Texas, unknown distributor. $45-55.

#701/2, 6" Rose Bowl, Stiegel Green, is used for this lamp. This lamp and the one in the following photograph were found in Michigan. Remember to look high and low, unknown distributor. $45-55.

#701/2, 6" Rose Bowl, Amber, is another example of the Rose Bowl being used in a lamp, Amber; unknown distributor. $45-55.

Reeded and Washington Bar Set

Bar Set, #701, 4" Reeded Jars, with Chrome Lid; #699, Washington, Square Cologne bottles with condiment spouts. Imperial sold a variety of glass products to metal companies for use in the secondary market. This set is placed here; it also belongs in following Washington pattern group, as well as the Reeded; could have been put in the Private Mould Customers; unknown distributor. $90-110.

Reproduction of Reeded

In the late 1990s, Fenton reproduced a 7 1/4" Vase with a crimped collar. The collar has the distinctive ruffle used on many Fenton items. This vase was made in Dusty Rose for Tiara Party Plan.

7 1/4" Dusty Rose Boudoir Vase, Crimped Neck, Fenton Art Glass for Tiara Party Plan, circa 1990s. Not Priced.

Washington, #699, AKA Mt. Vernon, Early American, and Lincoln

In 1920, Phillip Eberling joined Imperial Glass Company. Before arriving at Imperial, he had designed the American pattern for Fostoria Glass Company. At Imperial, Mr. Eberling was assigned to design a product to compete with the Fostoria American pattern. The result was design #699, originally known as Mt. Vernon.

Just prior to Imperial's new design introduction, Cambridge Glass Company had applied for a patent of its new design named Mt. Vernon. Cambridge was awarded the rights to the Mt. Vernon name. Since Imperial had already placed orders for catalogs that included the new pattern named Mt. Vernon, Imperial received permission to issue the catalogs with the conflicting name. Later Imperial changed the pattern name to Washington.

In 1934, the round base design on the stems was changed to a square base. The Washington pattern was discontinued in 1948.

When Imperial sold the Washington pattern to Butler Brothers in 1938, it was given the name "Early American." This only adds to the confusion of Imperial identification of this pattern name. For a short time, Imperial Glass even referred to the pattern as Lincoln.

As you read the list of Washington items sold to Butler Brother in 1938, remember that Imperial used the same shapes in many of its patterns. It will be repeated often in this book that no list of items produced is to be considered a complete list. More items were added as the years passed. The material given here is only a brief look at only a small part of Imperial's production that spanned eighty years.

We are giving the list of Washington sold to Butler Brothers as it is the most complete list of Washington production that we have.

#6990D, 8" Salad Plate
#699, 12 oz. Ice Tea
#6992, Goblet
#6992, Sherbet
#699, 6" Pickle, 2-handle
#6991W, 5" Butter Tub, tab handles
#6991, 5 3/4" Nappy, 2-handle
#6990W, 7" Bowl
#699, 5 3/4" Bon Bon, 1 handle
#6990N, 5" Lily Bowl
#6998D, 12" Plate, pointed edge
#699, 10 1/2" Celery Tray
#6998A, 9" Salad Bowl
#6995, 5 3/4" Preserve, 2-handle with cover
#6990, 5" Candy Box with cover
#6990, Sugar and Cream Set
#6997D, 11" Cake Plate, pointed edge
#6996F, 8" Shallow Nappy
#699, 7 1/4" Square Relish
#699F, 6" Comport
#6997B, 8 1/2" Berry Bowl
#6991, 6" Vase, smooth edge
#69910V, 13 1/2" Serving Plate, smooth edge
#699, Salt and Pepper Set, non-corrosive metal tops, guaranteed
#6996, 54 oz. Lipped Ice Jug
#6999B/749, 3-pc. Console Set, 10" 3-toed bowl with 4 1/2" candleholders
#6998B, 4 pc. Salad Set
#6993, 10" Vase, pointed edge

#69911, 6 qt., Punch Set; Bowl; Flat Plate, Cups. $100-125.

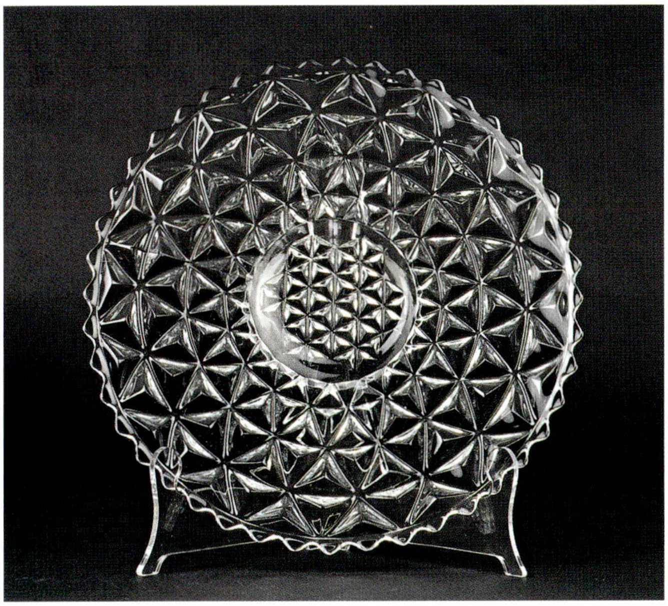

#699/7D, 11" Plate, note center ring. $12-17.

#699, 2-Tier Tidbit, Plates 9" and 11", top chrome post with a 2" circle handle. $25-35.

#6993, 10" Vase. $20-25; Similar #6991, 6" vase can also be found. $15-20.

#699, 4 1/2" Jelly. $10-15; #699F, 6" Compote. $12-15.

#6990, Open Sugar and Cream. $10-12 each.

#6992, 3" Candleholder, square. $45-50 each.

#6990N, 5" Flower Bowl, cupped, straight top. $25-30.

#6696N, 6" Lily or Nut Bowl. $15-20; also produced was a #6997N, 7" Lily or Nut Bowl, $15-20; #6998N, 8" Lily or Nut Bowl (notice the pointed edge). $15-20.

#6995D, 8" Plate, square. $8-10.

#699, Cruet, (A taller, pointed stopper is the one usually found in this cruet.) $15-20.

#6996N, 6" Lily Bowl,(note saw tooth edge), attached metal base. $20-25.

#699, 10" Celery Tray. $25-30.

#699, 5" Butter Tub. $30-35.

699F, 6 " Comport. $12-15.

#699, Cologne. $15-20.

#699, Salt and Pepper. This set was found by friends just before the book was finished. It is the only set we have seen. $20-22.

#6992, Goblet, Ritz Blue. $12-15.

#699, Vase, 6", Ruby. $35-40.

The following three photographs of the 7" Washington Vase could only be found in 1958 catalog pages issued between catalogs. Remember that this pattern was originally designed in the late 1930s and was called Mt. Vernon for a short period before being renamed.

#699, Vase, 7", Yellow. $25-30.

#699, Vase, 7", Pink. $25-30.

#699, Vase, 7", Green. $25-30.

The next photographs show the 5" Washington Vase without the large base that is shown in the previous photographs. The 5" Vase is made using the cologne bottle mould and then crimping the neck.

#699, Vase, 5", Blue. $15-20.

#699, Vase, 5", Yellow and Green. $15-20.

#699, 5" Vase, Turquoise. $15-20.

The rest of the Washington Photographs could have been in the Private Mould Customers, but again, we felt that they would be better served here.

#699, Powder Box, decorated metal lid, (no information on metal manufacturer) $35-40.

#699, Powder Box, decorated metal lid , another view (no information on metal manufacturer). $35-40.

#699, Powder Box with Cover, 3 1/2"; #699, Cologne with matching metal, (no information on metal manufacturer). $25-30 each.

The dresser set in the following photograph is a combination of two Washington Colognes with a Fostoria American powder box. There have been two of these sets found. As a reminder, Phillip Eberling designed the Washington pattern for Imperial after he designed the American pattern for Fostoria Glass Company; unknown distributor.

#699, Colognes with a Fostoria American Puff Box. $225-250.

#699, Shade, Carnival; this shade in Crystal is a documented item. It is unknown if the carnival shade is an Imperial original or if it is a reproduction. The documented Crystal shade is much thinner glass than the carnival shade. Some of Imperial's lampshade moulds were sold to companies in Mexico; we have no printed information on any use of these moulds. $45-50.

The #699, 10" Lamp, Vase with the plain edge; unknown distributor. $75-85.

The #699, 6" Lamp, 6" Vase for comparison, unknown distributor. $50-55.

#699, Lamp, Bowl, Compote with foot cut off. $85-95.

#55692VE, AKA #699, 10" Bowl, Verde, Star Exclusive, 1977, (discussed in Private Mould Customers). $12-15.

New Rochelle, #474- 1915

For the most part, Imperial always referred to the pattern #474 by only the number. It was dubbed New Rochelle in one early catalog. The distinguishing part of this design is the depressed petals of the flower. In 1915, the pattern began with an estimated 25 pieces and was discontinued in 1927. A few pieces appeared again in the 1967 Collectors Crystal group.

12" Footed Vase
1 qt. Pitcher
Table Tumbler
13 oz. Tavern Tankard
Butter and Cover

Space does not permit naming exactly when all patterns and all items were produced. Generally collectors are more interested in being able to identify some of the less known patterns made by Imperial Glass.

#699, 10" Bowl, Cobalt, Reproduction by L.E. Smith Company? Not priced.

In 1966 to 1968, the #474 Tankard Mug was made in Rubigold and Peacock Carnival. The #4743 Pitcher, and Tumbler were made in Crystal, and the #474C Compote and #474 Goblet were made in Antique Blue. Carnival prices will be considerably higher. A good reference is *Imperial Carnival Glass*, Collector Books, author Carl O. Burns.

#4743, Pitcher, 1/2 Gallon. $35-45; Tumblers. $12-15.

#474, Punch Bowl and Cups. $75-90.

#474, Carnival Punch Cup. $12-15; The #474 Cup was made in Marigold in the early years and again in later years it was produced in Rubigold. The later cup should have the IG in the bottom of it, but we had not seen one that is marked.

#474, 6 1/2" Carnival Vase, Peacock. $45-50.

#474, Heather Covered Candy, Heather. $35-40.

#474, Salt Shaker, note the lid is plastic; the metal is cemented to the neck of the shaker. $12-14.

#474, Top row, 9" Bowl, round, $20-25; 9 1/4" Bowl, square, $25-30; Bottom row, 9 1/2" Relish, oval, $15-20; Salt and Pepper. $20-25.

#474, Oval Relish. 9 1/2". $15-20.

#474, Cologne Bottle, Wide Neck. $55-60. A jar of this size and shape would have often been called a Lavender Jar. It is not documented as far as we know. Perhaps it was a private mould item. #474, Cologne Bottle, Crystal, metal unknown distributor. $30-35.

#474, Powder Box, Horizon Blue Carnival, Peacock Carnival, Marigold Carnival. $35-40 each; Crystal. $20-25.

#474, Light Shade, viewed from the side of the depressed flower petals. $45-50. The #474 Lamp Shade also comes in Helios Carnival. $100+.

#474 Light Shade, viewed from opposite side of the depressed flower petals. $45-50.

#474, Cologne, Top, Crystal, $25-30; Mustard, Pink, Turquoise. $30-35.

Pillar Flute, #682: 1936-1945

Pillar Flute is another of the more plentiful groups among the smaller patterns. The sparkle in the crisp clearness of the glass in the Pillar Flute Rose Bowl must have been the reason the vase was a favorite flower container. Imperial used the Rose Bowl shape in several patterns during the late 1930s and early 1940s. Ruby, Viennese Blue, Amber, and Crystal were early colors of production of Pillar Flute. During this same time period, other patterns were made in Hock Green, Transparent Gold, Meadow Green, Ritz Blue, Stiegel, Moonstone, Black, Rose Pink, and Topaz. It seems reasonable to think that almost any of Imperial's patterns could be made in these colors.

Candleholders for Pillar Flute and other small patterns will be shown in the Candleholder section. The following list was taken from a 1938 Price List:

#6825A, 6" Round Bowl
#6825B, 6 1/2" Bowl
#6820W, 7" Bowl
#6827B, 8 1/2" Bowl
#682S, 5 1/2" Bowl
#6823D, 6" Plate
#6820D, 8" Plate
#6825D, 10 1/2" Plate
#682S, 8" Plate
#682, 8 1/2" Celery Tray
#682B, 4 1/2" Footed Jelly
#682, 4 1/2" 1-handled Nappy
#682, 4 1/2" 2-handled Nappy
#682/2, 6 1/2" 2-handled Relish
#682, 6" 2-handle Pickle
#682, 6" Vase
#6825N, 5" Lily Bowl
#682F, 7" Comport
#682, Cup & Saucer
#682, Sugar and Cream set

#6825N, 5" Rose Bowl. $20-22.

#682, Chandelier with 5 arms; glass part matches the sketch of articles Imperial produced for Lightolier Lighting Company. $75-100.

#682, 5 1/2" Cigarette Box and 3 3/4" Square Ash Trays; this set was made for Butler Brothers in 1940, but we feel it is more important to show here than in Private Mould Customers. It was also made for Irving W. Rice. The shield label on this set indicates this set was made for Irving W. Rice. $50-55 set.

#682F, Bowl, shallow, footed, without metal, Ruby. $15-20.

#682F, 7" Dish, shallow, footed, metal handle, Ruby. The metal distributor is unknown. (This piece was an early acquisition for examples for this book. It was an appreciated house gift from a thoughtful couple.) $25-35.

#6828B, 10" Bowl; #682F, 7" Compote, with metal and Viennese Blue. $25-35. It seems that when you acquire one example, a second one is soon to be found. Only months after receiving the Ruby dish in the previous photo, we found this one in south Texas. The metal distributor is unknown.

#6828B, 10" Bowl; snap bottom, sterling base, unknown distributor. $35-40.

#6827B, 9" Flared Bowl, Ruby. $35-40.

.#682, 6 1/4", 2 Handled Pickle, Marigold Carnival. $20-25.

#682, Pillar Flute Cologne, made for Irice. $30-35

#682, Pillar Flute Cologne, Ruby Flashing, unknown distributor. $30-35.

Laced Edge AKA Lace Edge, #780, #749, #745, #743: 1930s-1960s

Imperial's Laced Edge design may be the third most popular Imperial pattern that is collected. Illustrated here is only a brief look at the variations of Laced Edge

Laced Edge was the name assigned by the Imperial Company, but the name was eventually shorted to Lace Edge by collectors and glass dealers. We prefer the original name especially since there is a Depression Glass pattern named Lace Edge. This has often led to confusion.

In 1942, salesmen were notified to "make no commitments on any of the Laced Edge items. We are very near closing a contract for a nation wide contract under a private label on this complete line." This statement was in reference to a 1943 pending contract with Sears Roebuck & Company of over 50 pieces of Laced Edge in the elegant Crystal under the pattern name "Crocheted" as it was to be labeled.

Laced Edge has a distinctive open loop edge and comes in a variety of shapes and colors. There are different design treatments to the outside surfaces. Laced Edge #749 has small triangular shapes on the body. The #745 has protruding dot areas with small points. Vertical optics is the side design of the #780. Another design is the #743, with symmetrical points. More examples of these side designs will be shown in the color section. Some of the colors of Laced Edge are; Sea Foam Green, Moonstone Blue, Amber, Green, Crystal, Stiegel Green, Ritz Blue, Rose Pink, Burgundy, Caramel Slag, and Verde.

Only a few items will be shown now and more examples will be shown in the section of Imperial colors. *Imperial's Lace Edge* Schiffer Publications, Ltd. by Laura Marsh thoroughly covers this pattern.

The next two items represent another example of the dual choice of placement in this book. These items could have been in the Unique Section, but we felt that Laced Edge collectors would prefer seeing them in this pattern group.

#7805F, 6 1/2" Compote, Silver Overlay. $25-35;#780B, 6 1/2" Bowl, shallow, Silvalyte Company Decorator. $25-35.

First is the clock. It became a part of our collection in a special way. We were presenting an Imperial Boudoir program in Pittsburgh, Pennsylvania to the local glass club. A gentleman was all smiles as he unwrapped this great clock and asked if we had one. He was so pleased to see our excitement as he put it into our hands. In a few minutes, the clock was ours. It is a very special piece to us. Since the clock was made for Irice in 1940s, it could be placed in the Private Mould Customer section, but we considered it more appropriate in the Laced Edge Section.

Second is the following mirror; it does not have the open design of Laced Edge, but it does have the scalloped edge. A friend found the first one of these while we shopped our way to the 2006 National Imperial Glass Collectors' Society Convention in St. Clairsville, Ohio. The mirror had the Irice black and silver label that resembles a shield. This was the necessary clue the collector friend needed to send her husband to their vehicle to retrieve our book, *Imperial's Boudoir, Etcetera.* They found the sketch of it on page 98. According to Imperial's records, the mirror was called a Laced Edge Mirror and was made for Irving W. Rice.

M163, Clock, 4", made for Irving W. Rice, 1940s. It was first shown in *Imperial's Boudoir, Etcetera* © 1996 by Myrna and Bob Garrison. $125-150.

As is customary with the authors and these friends, one will tell the other envious collector, "the next one is yours." The second mirror was found 15 minutes later, only one block away from the first great find. WHAT EXCITEMENT.

M-163, Mirror, 7", made for Irving W. Rice, 1940s. Back view shows stand. $125-150.

#780, Lamp, 4-Toed Vase. This little vase dates in the late 1930s. Three collectors have found these lamps in various parts of the country. A fellow collector and the authors believe when two or more of altered items appear in distant locations, they are not homemade but probably are the result of an after factory adaptation. Unknown distributor. $45-50,

#7455B, 6 1/2" Nappy, Belled, Sea Foam Green. $20-25.

#11/7455B, 6 1/2" Bowl, on left. $8-10; #1950/78C, 6" Candleholder. $10-12; right, 1950/274C, 7" 4-Toed, Comporte, Milk Glass. $15-20.

#749, 6" Bowl, Sea Foam Blue. $30-35.

#743, 4 1/2"-5 1/2" Vases, 4-Toed, various colors, Green, Ruby, Ritz Blue, Sea Foam Blue, Smoke, and Amber. $15-35.

"Molly," #725, #742, #741: 1930s & 1940s

A short line #725, labeled "Molly" in earlier research by some authors, has been of interest to a few collectors. Following are some photographs to give collectors a glimpse at this pattern. Only a luncheon set can be built. #725 was produced for Imperial's general line in Crystal and Ruby. In 1940, a few items were made in Venetian Blue, also for the general line of Imperial. #725 was made in Black and decorated with the Cosmos for Butler Brothers in 1937.

#7257/3B, 9" Bowl, Ruby. $25-30; #7257/3D, 10 1/2" Plate, Ruby. $25-30; Other colors are Rose Pink, Sea Form Green, Sea Foam Blue. Some items in this pattern were made with the Intaglio bottom for Butler Brothers in 1940. Please refer to Private Mould Customers for more information of the relationship between Butler Brothers and Imperial Glass.

#7255, Mayo Set, 7 1/4" Bowl, Ruby. $20-25; 7 1/4" 2-handled Nappy; 2-handled Plate, 7 1/4", Ruby. $20-25.

#725, Bowl. $12-15; #7255D, Plate. $12-15; #7257 Cup and Saucer, Ruby. $12-15.

#725/6 Sugar and Cream; notice the square edge handles that Imperial used on many of its designs, Ruby. $25-30.

#725, Place Set: 7285D, 8" Plate, Cup, Saucer; Sea Foam Green. $35-40.

725E, Handled Plate with 2 Sides Up. $20-25; 2-handled Plate, Ruby. $20-25.

Nucut: 1914-1936

In 1914, Imperial applied for a patent for the trade name, NUCUT. The first piece of Nucut was the #453, Handled Nappy. This line grew to 102 items and was discontinued in 1936.

Collectors Crystal- 1953-1984

The first catalog we have that features Collectors Crystal is the 1953 catalog.When Collectos Crystal began, it was labeled #282. When the pattern was made in different colors, it might have a mold number that relates to the color group. According to one factory note, "In 1967, ten more Nucut items were reissued and dubbed Collectors Crystal. It was launched with a large sale to F. W. Woolworth." It contimued to be featured in catalogs until the last catalog in 1982-1983. So often, when a person refers to "Collectors Crystal" they think that it is a pattern of one design, but it is a reissue of the several early pressed items from the original group of items named Nucut.

A 1965, Price List had 41 items in the Collectors Crystal group. It also stated that the moulds were 50 years old. In the 1980s, before the factory closed the number of items in the Collectors Crystal line had increased to fifty-eight. The numbering of items indicates there are several different groups of patterns that comprise this group.

81, 5" Aladdin Lamp Handled, Candleholder
212, Sugar and Cream Set
292, 3 1/2" Handled. Candle Bowl
302, 13 oz. Handled. Cordial Bottle
349, 22 oz. Liquer [sic] Bottle
404D, 12" Plate
404F, 10 1/2" Shallow Bowl
466/1, 11 1/2" Celery Tray
474, 12" Footed Vase
474, 1 pt. Pitcher
474, Table Tumbler
474, 12 oz. Tavern Tankard
503, 6 1/2" Oval Nappy
505, 8" Footed Vase
505, 6 1/2" Tall 2-handled Celery Vase
505, 9 1/2" Footed Cake Stand
505C, 7" Crimped Compote
511, 5 3/4" Footed Compote
536, 6" Vase
541, 6" Heart Nappy
555, 4 1/2" Footed Compote
564, 8" Pickle
568, 5" Handled Nappy
607, 10" Oval Candle Bowl
612, Salt and Pepper
612, 8 1/2" Crimped Vase
612, Decanter and Stopper
612, Wine
612, Cordial
678, 3 pt. Pitcher
678, 9 oz. Tumbler
737A, 8 1/2" Footed Bowl
2920, 2-pc. Handled Candlelamp 10 1/2" Tall
4021, 4 1/2" Footed Jelly
4022, 6 1/2" Footed Compote
5057, 8" Bowl
5057D, 10 1/2" Plate
5059, 10" Bowl
5059C, 11" Crimped Bowl
5059D, 13" Plate

Collectors Crystal pieces were produced in a variety of colors. In addition to Crystal, there was Fired Gold on Crystal, Rubigold, Peacock Carnival, and Decorated Cranberry.

Most of the Nucut items were made in Crystal and were in the 1930s or earlier. We included them in the Collectors Crystal group since the design matched the #282 Biscuit Jars that are a part of the Collectors Crystal Group.

#2820A, 4 1/2" Handled Berry. $15-20.

#282, Salt and Pepper, $50-55; #2827C, 8 1/2" Bowl, $15-20; #282D, 11" Plate. $15-20.

#2820B, 5 1/2" Bon Bon, handled. $25-30; #282, Tall Celery. $35-40; #28250, 6" Spoon Tray; early items. $25-30.

#2820, 12" Banana Dish. $35-40; #2825E, 6" Green Onion, without handles, early items. $25-30.

#282, Whisky Bottle, missing stopper; comes with pressed or cut stopper, early item. $45-50.

#2820S, 4 1/2" Olive, Square, early item. $30-35.

#282, Tall Celery, note smooth edge; #282, Tall Celery, note small scalloped top edge. $35-45.

#2820A, 4 1/2" Handled Berry, $15-20; #282, 10 oz. Goblet, $12-15; #282, Creaner, $15-20.

#282, Pitcher, 8 1/2" tall. $85-95.

Imperial Vintage Ruby, #473

Presented here is another pattern made in a limited number of pieces for collectors who want a small luncheon set. It is a beautiful Ruby (prefix #10) and is from the popular grape design moulds.

The glass is golden in the center or base and then runs into a dark Ruby at the outer edges. This is often referred to as Amberina. To produce Ruby glass, there has to be a second firing of the glass while it is in the finishing process. The second firing has to be at an extremely high temperature. If the temperature is not reached, the color is a Yellow to Amber variant rather than overall Ruby.

#10/880, 3 1/2" Candleholders. $12-15; #474, Bowl, Crimped. $20-25.

#10/831, Sugar and Cream. $20-25.

#10/473, 6 oz. Sherbet. $15-20; back #10/5D, 8 1/2" Dessert Plate. $8-10; front 10/6D, 9 1/2", Dinner Plate. $15-20; Cordial. $15-20; #4737, Cup and Saucer. $12-15.

#10/310, Bud Vase. $15-20; #10/810, Candy Jar, footed (missing lid). $15-20.

Olive, #134: early 1930s

Olive is designed with depressed circles and some items have a base design consisting of small lines. Olive is similar to Old English. Old English has the same depressed circles and it has depressed oblong elements. Colors available were Hock Green, Ritz Blue, Ruby, Amber, and Venetian Blue. The following list is taken from a 1937 price list:

#1346A, 3-pc. Console Set
#134, 2 1/2" Candlestick
#1346A, 9" Comport
#1346N, 7" Rose Bowl
#1346N, Bowl and Holder
#13441/2F, 6" Comport
#134, 3-pc. Mayonnaise
#134, Candy Jar and Cover
#1344D, 6" Plate
#1345D, 8" Plate
#1348D, 12" Plate
#134, Cup and Saucer
#134, Sugar and Cream
#615, Ladle

Usually we think of comports having a stem, but this is not always the case. Generally, Imperial named like shapes the same name in most lines. Of course, there are variations to this naming of items.

#134, 7 1/2" Candy Jar and Cover. $35-40; #1346B, Flared Bowl, Ruby. $20-25.

#13441/2B, 6" Comport, Amber. $15-18. In the Olive line, flared bowls and shallow bowls are called comports.

#1346A, 9" Comport or Pretzel Bowl. $30-35. #134, 2 1/2" Candle Sticks, Viennese Blue. $15-20.

According to Encarta Dictionary, "compote as a noun is stewed fruit and it is also a glass dish with a long stem, used for serving fruit, nuts, or candy." This definition tells us that a compote is the fruit and it, also tells us it is a dish that holds the fruit. Comporte and compote are used interchangeably.

#134, 7 1/2" Candy Jar and Cover, Ritz Blue, unknown metal distributor. $40-45.

#134, Candle Stick, 2 1/2". $15-20; #1346N, 7" Rose Bowl, Ruby. $25-30.

Empire, #779: late 1930s

The following section will alert collectors to the Empire pattern and the items that might be found in this pattern. The line originated in the late 1930s. Over 20 items were listed on a 1938 price list. Viennese Blue, Amber, Meadow Green, and Ruby were some of the documented colors.

#7796, 3" Candlestick
#7796A, 7 1/2" Round Bowl
#7796W, 8" Flared Bowl
#7796D, 10" Plate
#7796N, 6" Cupped Lily Bowl
#7796SC, 9" Fancy Square Bowl
#779, 4" Footed Ash Tray
#779, Candy Box and Cover
#779, Individual Salt
#779S, 8" Square Bowl
#779S, 11" Plate, Square
#779S, 2-pc., Square Salad Set
#779S, 4 pc. Square Salad Set
#7796N, 6" Flower Bowl with Wire Rack
#779, 5" Dolphin Candlestick
#779S, 3-pc. Console Set
#779S, 3-pc. Mayonnaise Set
#779S, 4 1/4" Square Fruit
#779S, 6" Square Plate
#779, 2-pc. Canapé Set
#779, 9" Round Tray
#779, 9" Relish, Oval
#7799D, 13" Plate
#7799V, 12 1/2" Plate
#7799W, 11" Bowl
#7799N, 9" Flower Bowl
#779, Sugar and Cream Set

Also, on this 1938 paper was a hand written note, "Special Customer #7796-0 Basket Bowl 9" x 5 1/2". Interestingly, we found this bowl before we found the notation.

#7796-0, 9 x 5 1/2" Basket Bowl. $25-30.

#779S, 7" Plate, square, Viennese Blue. $12-15.

#779, Cologne. This item is rather scarce. $75-85.

#779, Condiment Set, 3" Bowl, square; hangtag for Continental Silver Co. Inc. New York, Chromium Plate. Imperial labels on bowls indicate early 1930 production. After 75 years, the set and labels are still in mint condition. This is another special house gift brought to us by a friend. $45-50.

#7796N, 6" Lily Bowl with metal. $40-45. #779, 5" Square Candleholder. $15-17 each.

Boudoir Lamp, Empire glass part. Imperial Glass Corporation made many parts for several different lamp companies. Some of the parts are actual items from the general line and other items resemble a pattern the company produces. When comparing this part with a piece from the Empire line, it definitely seems to be the same design. $35-40.

Hobnail, AKA Early American Hobnail, #741, #742, & #749, #724: 1930s-1960s

Imperial had two designs referred to as Hobnail. The largest group had a small smooth, raised bump #741, #742, and #749. There was also had a pattern referred to as Pointed Hobnail, #724.

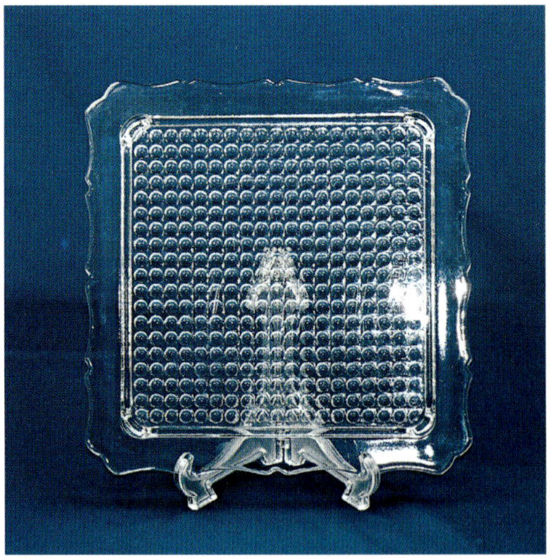

#742, Cake Plate. $25-30.

#742, 4 1/4", Vase, Ultra Blue, Green, Pink, Forget-Me-Not Opaque is an example of how Imperial used a mould for several different colors; $20-25. This vase was originally the bottom for a cologne bottle. The same mould would have been used for a vase as for the cologne. The varied shapes would be the result of a different neck technique applied by the finisher.

#742, 6 1/2", Ivy Ball, Sea Foam Green, Sea Foam Blue, and Dew Drop Stamm House. The Dew Drop is often mistaken for a Fenton Art Glass product. Imperial's Stamm House was produced in 1966 and consisted of many designs. $40-45 each.

#742, 6 1/2", Ivy Ball, Pink, Green. $30-35.

#742, 6 1/2" Ivy Ball, Crystal. $20-22.

#742, 6 1/2" Ivy Ball, Black. $35-40.

#742, 6 1/2" Ivy Ball, Stiegel Green, Ruby, Ritz Blue. $35-40, each.

#1950/188, 6 1/2" Ivy Ball, Glossy Milk Glass; 1952/188, 6 1/2" Ivy Ball, Doeskin, Milk Glass. $25-30 each.

#201, H. 12 " Hand Lamp, Verde. $75-80; #114, 7 1/4" Lamp Vase, Verde. $25-30.

#201, H. 12" Hand Lamp, Hobnail, Ultra Blue. $55-65; #114, 7 1/4" Lamp Vase, Hobnail, Ultra Blue. $30-35.

#201, 12" Stamm House Lamp, footed, Dew Drop Opalescent. $200-250.

#742, Hobnail Cologne Bottle, matching stopper, Sea Foam Blue. $70-75. Other colors to be found are Ritz Blue. $60-65, Rose Pink. $35-40, Imperial Green. $35-40, Crystal. $20-25.

#742, Hobnail Cologne Bottle, clear stopper is debatable, Ruby. $70-75.

Monticello, AKA Salem #698: 1922-1930s

Monticello #698 is similar in design to A.H. Heisey's Victorian pattern. Both designs are small raised squares.

We have no records of this, but we were told that some of the Monticello moulds were sold to a Mexico firm in 1948. We have seen nothing to indicate to us that these have been reproduced.

Thirty-nine items, depending on how you count pieces and sets, were made in Crystal. The following appeared on a 1937 price list for Salem.

#698, Basket, Round
#6985A, 6" Bowl, Round
#6986A, 7" Bowl, Round
#6987A, 8" Bowl, Round
#6988A, 9" Bowl, Round
#6985, 6 1/2" Bowl, Belled
#6986B, 7 1/2" Blow, Belled
#6987B, 8 1/2" Bowl, Belled
#6988B, 10" Bowl, Belled
#69810B, 12 1/2" Bowl, Belled
#698, 7 1/2" Bowl, Square
#69810D, 3-pc. Buffet Set
#69810V, 3-pc. Buffet Set
#6982, Candy Jar and Cover
#698, 9" Celery Tray
#698, Cheese and Cover
#698, Cocktail
#698F, 5 1/4" Comport
#698X, 5 3/4" Comport
#698, 4 3/4" Cream Soup, 2-handled
#6982, Cup and Saucer
#6982, Tea Cup
#6982, Saucer
#698, 4 1/2" Finger Bowl
#6987N, 7" Flower Bowl and Holder
#6983W, 5" Fruit, Flared
#6984A, 4 1/4" Fruit, Round
#6984B, 4 1/2" Fruit, Belled
#698, Goblet
#6981W, 5 1/2" Ice or Butter Tub
#6985N, 5" Lily Bowl
#6986N, 6" Lily Bowl
#6987N, 7" Lily Bowl
#6988N, 8" Lily Bowl
#698, 3-pc. Mayonnaise Set
#6980W, 7" Nappy, Flared
#6986F, 8" Nappy, Shallow
#6987F, 9" Nappy, Shallow
#6988F, 10" Nappy, Shallow
#698, 5 1/2 Nappy, one-handled,
#6988A, 4-pc. Salad Set 9" Round Deep Bowl; 12" Round Plate; #701, Spoon and Fork
#6980D, 8" Plate, Ruby (added to general line in 1938)
#698, 9 oz. Tumbler, Moonstone (added in 1938)
#698, Tid Bit Set, Crystal (added in 1938)

#698, 6" Oval Pickle Dish. $12-15.

#698, Cologne Bottle. $35-45.

#6986A, 7" Bowl. $12-15.

"Diamond Block," #330: 1930s

"Diamond Block" is a small diamond shape with incised sides and a raised dot at every point. The top edges are small saw tooth designs similar to other Imperial edge designs. In 1923, Woolworth had the exclusive rights to this pattern and according to a note in factory paper; it was Woolworth's best Imperial Glass seller. In 1928, Woolworth dropped the line and business between Imperial Glass Company and Woolworth was ending. Colors named were Pink, Green, Blue, and Crystal. We believe that Black was made during the 1930s, also. Following is an early list of items offered:

#3306B, 71/2" Berry
#330, 5 1/2" Honey Dish
#3305B, 6 1/2" Nappy
#330, 6" Tankard Jug
#330B, 5" Footed Jelly
#330, 8 1/2" Celery Tray
#330, Open Sugar
#330, Cream
#330, 4 1/2" Handled Jelly Dish
#3305N, 6" Lily Bowl
#330, 6 1/2" Pickle Dish
#330, 6" Bouquet

#3305N, 5" "Diamond Block," Lily Bowl, Black. $25-30.

#3305B, 6 1/2" Flared Bowl, Blue. $20-22.

#3305N, 5" Lily Bowl, Pink, Top $20-25; Left, #3305B, 6 1/2" Flared Bowl, Green. $20-22; Right 6 1/2" 2-handled Pickle, Yellow. $15-20.

Tradition, #165: 1930s

Tradition bears a close resemblance to Imperial's #160 Cape Cod line. It has the depressed circles and a diamond point band as does Cape Cod, but it is lacking the depressed large diamond around the depressed circles. In addition, the depressed circles are on the outside of the diamond point band—reverse to the Cape Cod pattern. Only nine items were offered in Tradition and over 300 items were offered in Cape Cod. Complete Cape Cod information is covered in *Imperial Cape Cod* ©2004, by Myrna and Bob Garrison, Schiffer Publishing Ltd.

Tradition colors that can be found are Heather, Bead Green, Green, Light Amber, Ruby, Turquoise, Pink, Blue Mist, Viennese Blue, Topaz, Mustard, and Milk Glass.

#165, 6 oz. Tradition, Juice, 6 oz. Sherbet. $5-7 each.

The Tradition line includes:

- #1655D, 8" Salad Plate
- #1655W, 7 1/4" Flared Nappy
- #1654 1/2A, 4 1/2" Finger Bowl
- #1654 1/2X, 6" Baked Apple
- #1655F, 7" Shallow Nappy
- #165, Lipped Ice Pitcher
- #165, 10 oz. Goblet
- #165, 6 oz. Sherbet
- #165, 12 oz. Iced Tea Tumbler
- #165, 7" Plate
- #165, Cocktail
- #165, Wine

Imperial Photograph.

Semi-Colonial #666, AKA "Cane" and "Huckabee" : 1918 through 1930s

The pattern #666 made its introduction in 1918 (there was conflicting information that placed this pattern in 1921). The four-piece tea set consisted of the covered butter, spoon holder, covered sugar bowl and cream pitcher were phased out in 1930. The last six items in this pattern were dropped in 1939.

#6660, Cream, Rose Pink. $35-40.

#666N, 6" Bowl. $20-30.

#666, 5" Bowl. $15-17.

#6661, 4" Powder Dish, Black. $25-30.

Colonial, #600, AKA "Chesterfield," and A.H. Heisey's Old Williamsburg #341

There was another little known event of name and design infringement. In 1920, the A.H. Heisey Company, Newark, Ohio entered a lawsuit against Imperial Glass Company for infringement of a patent design Heisey held on its #341 Old Williamsburg line. Heisey claimed that Imperial's #600 line AKA Colonial was copied after Heisey's #341 line.

Five years later the verdict was rendered in favor of Imperial. It was an expensive defense for the Imperial Glass Company. With the exception of two items, Imperial closed out the #600 line, in the 1930s. This was the second line to bear Imperial's Iron Cross trademark. The last of this #600 design to be used was a toothpick holder and a salt dip in the 1967 catalog.

It is ironic that thirty years later, Imperial would buy the moulds of the defunct Heisey Company and eventually reissue Heisey's Old Williamsburg line in Crystal as well as colors.

In the late 1950s, Imperial produced thirty-six items in Heisey's Old Williamsburg in Crystal. Collectors never seemed to be bothered by the question, "Is it by Heisey or Imperial Glass Corporation?"

#600, Rose Bowl or Nut Bowl. This bowl is from the original line #600. We do not have any paper that gives information about the mould number. $15-20.

In 1963, Imperial produced Old Williamsburg in Amber, Antique Blue, Azalea, and Verde. Blue Haze and Nut Brown followed in 1970s. Sunshine Yellow was made in 1974-1975 and Ultra Blue was next year. Rose Pink started in 1978 and last was Ruby and Evergreen in 1982-1983.

When we were in the factory during the final liquidation in 1985, an employee opened some doors to check what was inside the cabinet. Shock was written on our faces when we saw a large number of Rose Pink Old Williamsburg stems. Twelve each of those stems now compliment our wedding china.

#341, Pitcher, Ultra Blue. $50-55.

#34, Heisey's by Imperial Old Williamsburg; #341, 3 oz. Wines; back row, Nut Brown, Ruby, Amber, middle row, Antique Blue, Pink, Verde, Yellow and Ultra Blue. $10-12 each.

Cathay, #5000: 1949

According to a company memorandum, the introduction of the Cathay line was limited to "fifty-seven stores in fifty-seven cities in thirty-one states." The statistical note indicates the number of establishments, evidently elite stores, to be allowed to participate in the initial public sale of Imperial Glass Corporation's Cathay Crystal, set for Monday April 25, 1949.

"Cathay is not oily and/or slick. It is accomplished partly by mould construction, by sand and other abrasives, by heat and by acid." Every piece was covered by design patent. The object of this was to protect every piece from being copied. Even the word Cathay was protected in the glass business.

Cathay was designed by Virginia B. Evans. All pieces except the very small ones, are signed by Virginia B. Evans. It took six years to bring Cathay to market. The idea first began in 1943, followed by research, design, trials and all aspects of manufacture before it appeared to the public in 1949.

Imperial distributed to its sales representatives a fully illustrated advertising packet that consisted of forty-three pages of illustrations and facts. It contained 15 pages of detailed information, sketches of all items plus actual glossy prints of the items.

We can show only a sample of this line, but we believe the facts and the list of items will assist collectors in this outstanding work by Imperial Glass. We will not price items in factory photos.

Following is a list of the Cathay items:

5000 Concubine Book-Ends
5001 Pagoda
5002 Shang Candy Jar
5004 Yang and Yin Ash Tray
5005 Lung Ash Tray
5006 Butterfly Ash Trays
5007 Plum Blossom Ash Trays
5008 Peach Blossom Mint or Nut Set
5009 Dragon Candle Holders
5010 Junk Flower Bowl
5011 Wu Ling Ash Tray, see reproduction note
5012 Ku Ribbon Vase
5013 Pillow Candle Bases
5014 Bamboo Urn
5016 Fu Wedding Vase
5017 Egrette
5018 Pillow Cigarette Set
5019 Ming Jar
5020 Shen Console Set
5022 Fan Sweetmeat Box,see reproduction note
5024 Scolding Bird
5026 Phoenix Bowl
5027 Wedding Lamps
5029 Empress Book-Stops
5030 Lu-Tung Book Holders
5033 Candle Servants
5034 Candle Servants
5038 Celestial Center Piece
5085 Pavilion Tray

The Cathay moulds were used by Imperial to reissue some of the designs in other colors: Black with gold accents items were made in 1953. Cranberry Frosted and Verde were made 1964-1965. Jade production was 1980-1981. A few names of items in Black are as follows:

4/5022, Candy Box & Cover, Fan Shape Imperial Black Suede.

4/5022/Dec, Gold Imperial Black and Gold.

4/5026, Phoenix Bowl Imperial Black Suede 1953.

#5033, Candle Servants, Man. $100-110.

#5034, Candle Servant, Woman. $100-110.

#5018, Ashtray to the three piece Pillow Cigarette Set. $65-75.

Reproductions in Dusty Rose by Fenton Art Glass for Tiara Party Plan c. 1990.

5011 Wu Ling Ash Tray
5022 Fan Sweetmeat Box

#5020/3 Shen Console Set.

Following are Imperial factory photographs. 5012 Ku Ribbon Vase. $200-250; #5013 Pillow Candle Bases.

#5016 Fu Wedding Vase. $50-60; #5029 Empress Book Stop.

5020 Shen Bowl, 5020 Shen Candleholders.

Dynasty Jade Bamboo Urn, top; 5002 Shang Jar, left; 5026 Phoenix Jar, right.

This item is included here by the generosity of a fellow author. He has the only known set of Salt and Peppers that were intended to be a part of the Cathay line. They are not finished with the Cathay finish. They are not included in the list above but they did appear in one of the original photographs of the line. He offered these to be used in this book so that collectors would be aware of them.

Chapter 3
Imperial's Colors

Imperial used many of its moulds to make a large part of its production in various colors during the long history of Imperial Glass Corporation. Often, through the years, the chemical mixtures were varied by only small amounts and then given a new name.

We cannot attempt to give official color names to all the photographs. We have been told that often a change of color would have only a slight variation of chemicals. That makes it almost impossible to distinguish between some of the small changes in color. A few times, we found a new name with the previous name in parenthesis, which indicated it was only a name change. Building this book has been a huge challenge because it covers so many patterns, groups of items and specific unique items. However, it is only a fraction of the enormous production of Imperial Glass Corporation.

Occasionally, it is difficult to know exactly what color name one should label an item. Adding to the difficulty in identifying the colors is that the thinness and the thickness of some pieces cause the color to become lighter or darker. Lack of color catalogs or missing catalogs is another added problem in deciding which color name is appropriate. Other Imperial researchers have shared in this difficultly. We only hope that we have conveyed accurate information. "A mistake is evidence that someone tried to do something." Author unknown

We have not attempted to chart all of Imperial's color names. While working on this book we found a notation of "Smoky Chartreuse" and in parenthesis was the name Verde. That seems to explain why we are all confused when it comes to knowing what the color name is for particular items. To us, it seemed more important to bring to collectors information on some of the production items. It might be of interest to a collectors to know some of the early color names. In order to see the names easily, we will capitalize all color names as well as common ones.

#2 Topaz
#3 Stiegel
#4 Black
#5 Hock Green
#6 Ritz Blue
#7 Moonstone
#10 Ruby
#21 Meadow Green
#40 Amber
#64 Rose Pink
#80 Venetian Blue AKA Viennese Blue

Vases

The small 4-toed vase was made with four different collars—B slanted outward, K curved outward, N curved inward, X flat. These vases come with three different side designs. The plain panel is #780; the diamond point side is #743; the "daisy and button" side is #745.

This vase alone can become a collection because there are so many different colors to be found. Shown in the following photographs are only a few examples of the colors, sides, and collars.

From experience, we know that one way to find documentation on a questionable item is to include it in a book. If it is incorrect, you will hear immediately. For that reason, we are showing these vases with a basket weave design on out side.

This 4-toed vase has several of the characteristics of the Imperial Laced Edge Vase. It has the Laced Edge collar, the lines on the toes and the ray design on the bottom. The only detail that differs from the documented Imperial vase is the basket weave on the outside. Who made this vase?

There are two other questionable points. The Crystal vase has an odd crimp to the collar and the Jadeite is an unusual color for Imperial. However, there is one example of this color mentioned and that is the #1 Flower Pot that is mentioned on page 47.

#780N, Vase, 4-Toed, Stiegel Green. $15-20.

#780B, 4 1/2"-5 1/2", Vase, 4-Toed, Amber, #780K, Ritz Blue, #780K, Early Amber. $15-20 each.

#743X, Vase, 4-Toed, Amber, Light Green. $15-20 each.

#745, 3" Rose Bowl or Ivy Ball, Various colors, front, Rose Pink. $20-25; Ritz Blue. $25-30; Stiegel Green. $20-25; Sea Foam Blue. $25-30; Crystal. $12-15; Amber. $15-20. Add $10-15 for the original hanging chain.

#749-0, 9 1/2" Basket Bowl, Ritz Blue, (Only a general line number was found in our paper, but in another line the basket bowl mould number ended with a 0.) $50-55.

#749-0, 9 1/2" Basket Bowl, Ruby. $40-50.

#749-0, 9 1/2" Basket Bowl, Stiegel Green. $40-50.

#7805K, 3 1/2" Flower Bowl, Satin and Crystal, plain panel. $20-25.

#7802K, 3 1/2" Flower Bowl, Cranberry Stained, collar flared. $25-30.

#207K, 5" Flower Arranger, Amber; (Generally, this bowl should have a flower frog.) Complete. $30-35.

#749, 5 1/2" Laced Edge, Bowl, shallow with small lace openings, Sea Foam Blue; most Laced Edge has the large open lace work, but there are a few pieces that have a less open, elongated Laced Edge. "Kathy Blue" is name used by H. M. Weatherman. $25-35.

#745, 3 1/2" Ivy Ball, vertical collar, Ruby, Undocumented. $*.

#780K, Vase, 4-Toed, Stiegel Green. $30-35.

#780, 4-Toed, Amber. $20-25.

#745, Bowl, Amber. 6". $15-20.

Also, in the following photograph of the 4-toed vases is another one that we have not documented. This questionable one has an outside design of "fish scales." To the authors, this example is believed to be Imperial, as well. The scales are identical to those on the #142, 2-pc. Canapé set pictured in an early catalog. The plate in that set is in the shape of a fish and has a design of fish scales. Solutions to these, anyone?

Basket Weave Vase; top row, Black, Jadeite , front left, Sea Foam Green, front right, Sea Foam Blue; center front, Viennese Blue with Fish Scales. The Sea Foam colors are not identical in shades but are very close.

Another example of a fun thing to collect, is the #86 Vase in many colors of glass produced by Imperial Glass Company. There is one small imposter out in the glass world. It is the same size and most of the same design. However, it is not crimped at the top and the top has small raised pinheads around it.

#86, 5" Vase, Ritz Blue, Ruby Flashed, Bead Green, Burgundy, Heather, Midas. $12-15 each.

#86, 5" Vase, Yellow, Flask Brown, and Amber. $12-15.

#51754, 5" Vase, Green Satin. $15-25.

#457, Aurora Jewels, 5" Vase. $20-25.

#610, 7 1/4", Whisk Broom Wall Vine Vase, $25-30; #612, 8" Footed Vase, $25-30; Standing Vase, Heritage Blue. $20-30 each.

#610, 7 1/4", Whisk Broom Wall Vine Vase, $20-25; #612, 8" Footed Vase, $22-25; #613, 6" Bud Vase, Milk Glass. $15-18.

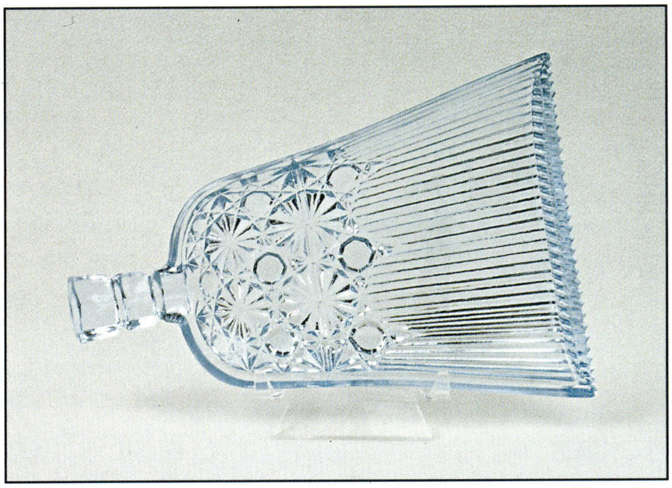

#910/1, 7 1/2" Whisk Broom Open Dish, Light Blue, #12-15.

#350, Vase, 5 1/2", South Jersey group, Stiegel Green Satin. $20-25.

The next three photos have rather peculiar numbers for Imperial. After Lenox purchased Imperial in 1973, they transferred identification numbers to computer numbers. The following items could have entirely different numbers from previous years.

Number changes occurred other times during years of production. When a mould was used in a different color and put into a different line of items, the number was often changed. We have used either the first numbers; the most often used numbers, or the number used for the particular item that is illustrated. It is just one of the variants over a period of eighty years of production.

#51735UB, 4" Ball Vase, left; #51747UB, 6" Bud Vase, right; 51746UB, 6" Bud Vase, back, Ultra Blue. $15-20 each.

Vases; 51746PL, 6" Bud Vase, left; #51744PL, 6" Meng Vase, right, Imperial Purple. $15-20 each.

#51745SY, 7 1/2" Li Po; 51744SY, 6" Meng; 51743SY, 5" Mei; 51747SY, 6" Bud Vase; 42749SY, 6-8", Swung Vase, Sunshine Yellow. $15-25 each.

Lamps

Collecting often happens accidentally. Once you have three items; e.g. lamps, candleholders, or baskets, you are on the road to collecting that item. The following photographs show examples of accidental collections.

The Bundling lamp is a copy of a lamp from another era. The name "bundling" is derived from that era. In pioneer days, boys and girls often shared room and beds. A board was placed down the center of the bed to prevent "bundling." Hence, a bundling lamp was burned in the room. Imperial's Bundling lamp was offered in a combination of colors as well as consisting of the same color for both pieces.

#216, 7 3/4" Grape Mini Oil Lamps, Sunshine Yellow with clear shade. $40-45; #216, 7 3/4" Antique Blue with matching shade. $50-60; #216, 7 3/4" Amber with matching shade. $40-45.

#9, 8 3/4" Bundling Lamp, Amber. $65-70; Lamp Vase, Grape, Amber. $20-25; #201H, 12-handled Lamp, Amber. $80-85; #216, 7 3/4" Boutique Lamp, Amber. $70-75; #201, 17", Peacock Feather, Honey Amber. $65-75.

#1886/114, 7 1/4" Lamp Vase, Dew Drop Opalescent. $35-45; #114, 7 1/4" Lamp Vase, Grape, Mustard. $30-40; #201H, 12" Handled Lamp, Mustard. $80-85.

#216, 7 3/4" Mini Lamp, Grape, Antique Blue. $50-60; #9 8 3/4" Bundling Lamp, Antique Blue. $65-75; #114, 7 1/4" Lamp Vase, Antique Blue. $30-35.

#9, 8 3/4" Bundling Lamp, Ultra Blue. $65-70.

#9, 8 3/4" Bundling Lamps, Ruby/Green. $60-65; Ruby/Milk Glass. $50-55; Satin/Green. $50-55, Amber/Crystal. $50-55.

#114, 7 1/4" Lamp Vase, Heather. $30-35; #9, 8 3/4" Bundling Lamp, Purple with Sueded Crystal shade. $70-75.

#216, 7 3/4" Mini Lamp Grape, Milk Glass. $40-45; #9, 8 3/4" Bundling Lamp, Milk Glass. $70-75; #216, 7 3/4" Mini Lamp Sueded Crystal. $40-45.

#350, 13" Lamp, Hobnail, Peacock, Carnival. $65-70.

#114, 7 1/4" Lamp Vase, Glossy Milk Glass; Doeskin Milk Glass. $25-27 each.

#201H, 12" Handled Lamp, Crystal. $75-85.

#201, 17" Lamp, Antique Blue, with decorated shade. $85-95.

#201, 17" Lamp, Antique Blue and Milk Glass. $85-95.

Slag

Mention of Imperial's slag will be limited to showing only an example of each color. For more information on Slag, Opaque and Milk Glass please check the book, *Milk Glass, Imperial Glass Corporation* ©2001, by Myrna and Bob Garrison. An outstanding source of Slag information can be found in *Slag and Marble Glass*, by Don Jennings and Nathan Taves, Schiffer Publishing, Ltd.

#720, (Lenox Number 43842), 5 1/2" Bell. $50-55; #1602, Cigarette Lighter, Cape Cod. $50-55, Purple Slag.

#661, (Lenox Number 43240), 5 1/2" Jar, Jade Slag. $65-75.

400/150, 6" Candlewick Heart; #43729, 6" Compote, Caramel Slag. $30-35.

#1776 (Lenox Number 43240), 4" Cigarette Holder, End of Day "Ruby Slag," $30-35.

#1601/8, (Lenox Number #43858), 6" Ash Tray, Caramel Slag. $20-30; 1601/8, (Lenox Number #43858), 6" Ash Tray, Blue Slag. $40-50.

Imperial facory photograph.

Hand-Painted Designs

Collectors will be able to transfer identification of one pattern shape to another pattern, one color name to another line, and one stroke of a brush to another decoration.

In 1943, Imperial produced "Southern Highlands" hand-painted designs on the #176 Stemware. The decorations were Fruit, Jonquil Aster, Lilac, and Tulip. The following notation was taken from Imperial records; "All decorations are excellent to tie in with the flat lines of the Southern Potteries having that decoration." Most likely one would be able to recognize one of these by the name description if you are familiar with the #176 Continental Line.

The #176, Continental Line was comprised of a Goblet, Saucer Champagne, cocktail, Wine, Cordial 14 oz. Tumbler, Oyster Cocktail (also numbered #3400), 80 oz. Pitcher and 40 oz. Martini Jug.

#7257, Compote, #615, Handled Relish, #820, Candleholder. $15-20 each.

#655, Vase, decorated with white/red flower with gold flowers and leaves. $20-25.

#7615B, 6 1/2" Bowl, 3-toed, flared out, left. $20-25; right, #7615N, 5" Lily Bowl. $20-25.

Another interesting notation in 1938, that we will only be able to share in words, is "Four Highly Fired Enamel Decorations; Tulip, Lily, Corn Flower, Lily of Valley." To our knowledge, we have no examples of this decoration. If you have a piece of Imperial with one of these decorations, this scrap of information may help date your item.

#734/75, Bowl, footed with Epergne insert similar to shape of the Cape Cod Epergne insert. The only difference is in the shape of the peg that fits into the bowl, Decorator unknown, possibility Imperial. $85-95.

Salad Bowl with Decorated #701 Fork and Spoon. $25-30. #5889, 10" Relish, Hand Painted by Imperial. $50-55.

Another example of Imperial's Hand Painting; good sample of Imperial's use of the yellow wheat stalk, red, and blue flowers.

It is exciting to be able to show you these two samples of Imperial's Hand Painting. This one is the corner of a clear glass tray decorated for Irice. We have references to these in our book, *Imperial's Boudoir, Etc*. There are no sketches to aid in recognition so it is our guess that this example is the A-139 Oblong Tray, Floral Spray, Decorated and Gold Border. Irice furnished the trays. $*.

We do not feel that we can match this to one of the seven existing numbers for these trays. The trays did come from a workers home and they might not have the documented designs on them. $*.

These are the #419 Pitchers from the Continental line. Imperial decorated many items from this line to complement patterns of pottery or to make up a set of decorated glassware for the Imperial Lines. On the right is Imperial's Susan design. We are unsure of the name on the left. We do know that the yellow flower is one of Imperial's designs.

Chapter 4
Decanters

Imperial Glass Company had a large demand for decanter bottles. We will share some of the outstanding decanters from Imperial's production. It would be virtually impossible to assemble examples of all the products of Imperial Glass Company to be shown in one or a group of books.

If you are in the East Central area of Ohio, be sure to visit the Imperial Glass Museum in Bellaire, Ohio. After many years, beginning in the early 1990s, of planning, dreaming and investigating many options, the museum was opened in 2003 by the National Imperial Glass Collectors' Society. A walk into this museum is a walk through the production history of the largest glass factory under one roof in the United States.

#544, Etiquette, Decanter. $85-95; 2 oz. Cordial. $12-15.

#163, Grape Decanter. $100-125; #473, Wine, Rubigold Carnival. $15-18.

#163, Grape Decanter. $100-125; #473, Cordial, Azure Blue Iridescent. $12-15.

#153, Swirl Vase. $15-20; #163, Grape Decanter. $60-75; #473 Wine, Milk Glass. $10-12.

#160/163, Cape Cod Decanter. $200-225; #160, Wines, Ruby. $20-25. We have seen two of these decanters with Ruby stoppers. All others have had crystal stoppers. We wish that we knew the rest of the story.

#160/163, Cape Cod Decanter, Ruby Flashed. $100-125; 1600 Wines. $18-25.

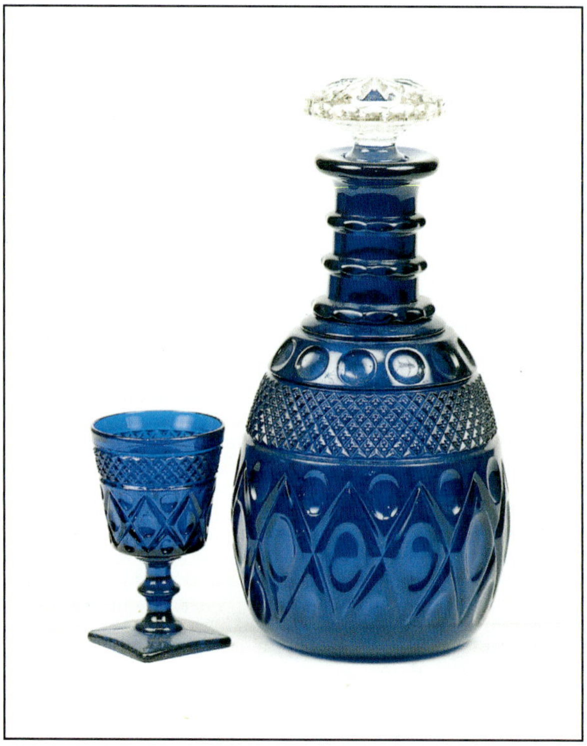

#160 Wine. $30-35; #160/63, Cape Cod Decanter, Ritz Blue. $225-250.

#G612, Collectors Crystal Decanter with Gold. $75-95;
#G612, Cordial. $12-15.

#41240, Wines, Mt. Vernon, Fired on Gold (decanter missing). $12-15.

#699, 36 oz. Decanter. $40-55;
2 oz. Cordial. $12-15.

#400/82, Candlewick, Bottle, Handled. $225-300.

#701, 36 oz. Reeded Shaker. $95-125; #701, 3 1/2 oz. Cocktail. $15-18; #701/3, 5" Bud Vase, Ritz Blue. $20-25.

Chapter 5
Cracker Jars

"Americana" Jars #282, AKA Cracker Jar; #282/1, AKA Milk Jar, Boudoir Jar, Nursery Jar: 1955-1979

This section is a prime example of a colorful collection that can be built while collecting only one design or one item. Displaying these jars on a kitchen counter or similar place can immediately brighten one's day. The owners of this outstanding collection made this section possible and gave much help and support during the research for this book.

This original #282 design was produced in 1913. It is variously called Cracker Jar, Americana Jar, or Biscuit Jar. The #282/1 (smaller size) has been called Milk Jar, Boudoir Jar and Nursery Jar. The #282 Cranberry Decorated in the most elusive one.

The following photographs will read left to right.

#282, Azalea. $60-70; Crystal. $25-35; Siamese Pink $55-65; in back; #282/1, front, Azalea $40-50; Crystal. $20-25; Siamese Pink. $35-45.

#282, Antique Blue $55-65; Mist Blue $45-55; in back; front, #282/1 Antique Blue $35-45; Mist Blue. $25-35.

#282, Blue Mist $45-55; Crystal $25-35; Antique Blue $55-65; Top, Azalea $60-70; Siamese Pink. $55-65.

#282, Verde $25-35; Mustard $45-55; Evergreen $55-65; front; back, Amber Glo $60-70; Amber $50-60.

#282, Verde $25-35; Mustard $45-55; Evergreen. $55-65; back; #282, front #282/1, Verde $20-25; Mustard; $25-35. Evergreen $35-45.

#282, Amber $60-70; 282/1. $40-50; #282, Amberglo; $50-60, #282/1; $25-35.

#282/1, Decorated Cranberry $35-45; missing from this group is the #282 Decorated Cranberry. $80-90.

#282, Turquoise Opaque, Glossy $50-60; 282/1. $40-50; #282 Turquoise Opaque, Doeskin $55-65; 282/1. $40-50.

#282, Forget-Me-Not Blue Opaque, Doeskin $55-65; #282, Forget-Me-Not Blue Opaque, Glossy $50-60. (The #282/1 Milk Jars are missing from photograph.)

#282, Midwest Custard Opaque, Doeskin $80-90; Midwest Custard Opaque, Glossy $80-90. (#282/1 Milk Jars are missing from photograph.)

#282, Milk Glass, Doeskin $55-65; Milk Glass, Glossy $50-60. (The #282/1 Milk Jars are missing from photograph.)

#282, #282/1, Peacock $45-55, $25-35; #282, #282/1, Marigold $45-55, $25-35; #282, #282/1, Helios Carnival $50-60. $30-40.

In 1904, the Milk Jar #1 was as early item from Imperial Glass Company. It has no knob on the lid. It is seldom seen and when it does appear, collectors confuse it with the #282/1 that has a lid with a knob on top.

#282/1, Milk Jar, with Lid from the Three-in-one, Yellow. $25-35.

#282/1, Blue Mist. $25-35; #1, No Knob. $25-35. (Jar is #282/1 and lid is Three-in-one.)

Three-in-one, Ruby. (This one really does not belong to this group but collectors always wonder about the similarity.) $80-90. (This can also be found in Crystal, Mustard Yellow, Verde Green, Amber, and Blue Mist.)

Chapter 6
Candleholders

Several of the candleholders could have been included in the previous pattern groups. By grouping the candleholders together, we thought it would illustrate a beautiful collection for one to build. It is also an opportunity to illustrate some pattern names that lack of information, and space does not permit detailed descriptions. The candleholders are priced individually unless otherwise noted. Some of the higher prices are due to their scarcity.

#643, Lenox #51783, Hobnail, 4" Candleholder, #51783, Ultra Blue. $20-25.

#682, Pillar Flute, Candleholder, circa 1940s. $40-50.

#1950/180, Milk Glass Leaf, Candleholder, 1952-1955. $15-20.

#46, Hoffman, Candleholder, Ruby. $20-25.

#90, Collectors Crystal Candleholder, Flat, $10-15; #81, 5" Handled Candleholder, footed. $25-30.

#220, Swedish Pinch, Candleholder, Hand-Painted. $35-50.

#414/1, Diamond Quilted, Candleholder, Rose Marie. $10-12.

#414/1, Diamond Quilted, Candleholder, Black. $15-20.

#78C, Laced Edge, Candleholder. $15-20.

#779, Empire, Candleholder. $15-20.

#779, Empire, Candleholder, Underneath View. $15-20.

#3031/2, Twisted Optic, 8 1/4" Candleholder, AKA, Swirl, Amber, (available in Rose Pink Green and Amber). $12-15.

#282, Collectors Crystal, Candleholder, Ruby. $25-30.

#1886, Stamm House, Candleholder, Round Bowl, Dew Drop Opalescent. $30-35.

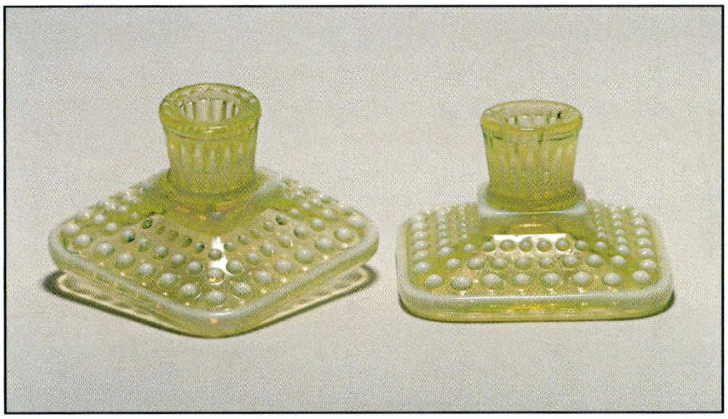

#1886/285, Stamm House, Candleholder, Square. $30-35.

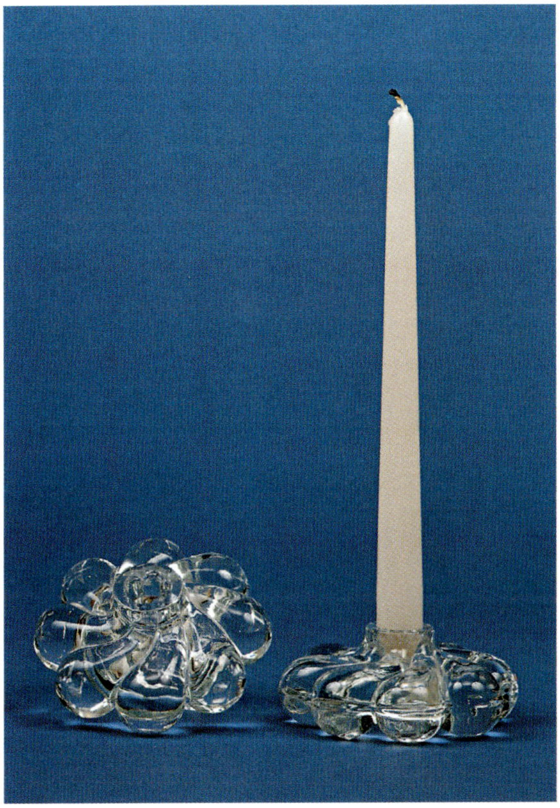

#E21, Elyslyn Label.

#E21, Elyslyn, Candleholder. $12-15.

1950/325, Candleholder, Glossy Milk Glass. $12-15.

#110/80 Twist, Candleholder. $35-45.

#41793, 5", Collectors Crystal. $20-15.

#13801, Old Williamsburg, Candleholder, Handled 5 3/8", $20-25; #341/2 (Lenox number 13790) 7 1/2". $20-25.

#42786 (Cambridge #1155), White Carnival, 3 1/2" Candleholder, from the Cambridge Everglade line mould, Marked IG and LIG. $15-20.

The following photograph will be of interest to Candlewick collectors. Often the #782 is thought to be Candlewick because of the beads on the sides of the candleholder. However, this candleholder does not have a Candlewick number or the usual bead design of Candlewick. It was produced during the early Candlewick era, but it was not included in the Candlewick line. The #782 with the side beads is preceded by the #169 candleholder that has no beads.

There is also a Green #782 Beaded Candleholder with a cut on it. We have not been able to find the name of this color or the date of production. Walter Lemiski, a fellow researcher and author of *Elegant Glass with Corn Flower Cut,* Schiffer Publishing, Ltd. brought a pair to us at the 2004 National Imperial Glass Collectors' Convention. What a great surprise!

#169 Candleholders, No Beads on Side, $15-20; #782 Candleholder, Side Beads. $25-35.

Only one piece of the Candlewick and Cape Cod lines is shown next. In either pattern, one could collect just candleholders. Check the bibliography for books that have photographs of Candlewick and Cape Cold candleholders.

#160/100, Cape Cod, Double Candleholder. $60-65

400/90, Candlewick, 4 1/2" Handled Candleholder, rim turned up more than most others. $*.

Chapter 7
Sets of Items

Christmas Plates: 1970-1981

Many sets of items are produced in limited editions that are collectable. Imperial produced an outstanding set of Christmas plates. The detail of the designs in these plates is exquisite. All twelve plates were made in a satin finish over crystal. In addition to the satin finish, each year a different color with an iridescent finish was produced. These beautiful plates were made from 1970 to 1981. Prices will average $20-25 for the Crystal Satin and $25-35 for the Iridescent finish.

Due to space limitations, we have chosen not to show these plates. We feel that the descriptions will guide you enough. When you read the words and see the subjects of the verse, you will know what you are admiring in your hands.

First Day of Christmas, 1970, Partridge in a Pear Tree, Blue, Satin Crystal
Second Day of Christmas, 1971, Two Turtle Doves, Green, Satin Crystal
Third Day of Christmas, 1972, Three French Hens, Amber, Satin Crystal
Fourth Day of Christmas, 1973, Four Colly Birds, White Carnival, Satin Crystal
Fifth Day of Christmas, 1974, Five Golden Rings, Verde Carnival, Satin Crystal
Sixth Day of Christmas, 1975, Six Geese-a-Laying, Yellow Carnival, Satin Crystal
Seventh Day of Christmas, 1976, Seven Swans a Swimming, Ultra Blue, Satin Crystal
Eighth Day of Christmas, 1977, Eight Maids A Milking, Nut Brown, Satin Crystal
Ninth Day of Christmas, 1978, Nine Drummers Drumming, Pink Carnival, Satin Crystal
Tenth Day of Christmas, 1979, Ten Pipers Piping, Horizon Blue Carnival, Satin Crystal
Eleventh Day of Christmas, 1980, Eleven Ladies Dancing, Meadow Green Carnival, Satin Crystal
Twelfth Day of Christmas, 1981, Twelve Lords-a-Leaping, Amberina, Satin Crystal

Christmas Ornaments: 1980

In 1980, Imperial introduced four of what was to be a twelve piece series of Christmas Ornaments. The first four ornaments are in the 1980 catalog. It was about that time that Imperial Glass began to experience financial problems. Factory paper does not show or mention the rest of this series.

It remains a mystery why there is a tenth day ornament existing. No ornaments after the number four were announced, however, there have been a few number ten ornaments found. We have found no mention of numbers five through twelve. Are there other Imperial Christmas ornaments from fifth to twelve in existence? The Island Mould Company in Wheeling, West Virginia, bought these moulds during the liquidation of Imperial. Maybe we will be fortunate enough to see another company finish this set with the fifth-twelfth day.

1st Day of Christmas, Blue Carnival; 2nd Day of Christmas, Amber; 3rd Day of Christmas, Green Carnival: 4th Day of Christmas, Crystal Carnival. 10th Day of Christmas. $15-25.

Colonial Bell: 1950s

This bell is made "off-hand," there is no mould used in making the bell. Colonial Bell, Stiegel Green, Bead Green. Other colors are Ruby, Madeira, and Antique Blue Burgundy. It is exciting to find one of these bells. Originally, a piece of cork held the ringer in place causing collectors to pass the bell thinking it was not in mint condition. $30-40.

Fish Canapés

These following party servers were made in the late 1930s, and were combined with the #142 Tumblers to complete the set. In addition to the fish set, the #142 was combined with other party trays. The most popular of these party trays was in the Candlewick line. Many companies bought the tumblers and applied different decorations. Collectors have found as many as fifty different cuts, etches, and hand-paintings to name some of the decorations.

It remains undetermined if Imperial made the #142 tumbler and sold it to other companies or if Imperial and other companies bought the #142 from an outside source. The #142 appears in an early catalog with the Imperial company logo in one corner and a reference of Old Central Quality in another corner. Imperial bought Central Glass Company in 1940. We have always felt the #142 may be a Central Glass product that was sold to several different glass companies.

#142, Fish Canapé and #142 Tumbler, Ruby, Amber, Ritz Blue, and Teal. $20-30.

#142, Fish Canapé, Satin Crystal and #142 tumbler, Satin and Star Edge; shown here is only one of the many possibilities of decorations. More examples of colors and decorations are show in *Candlewick: Colored and Decorated*, Schiffer Publishing, Ltd. by Myrna and Bob Garrison. $20-30.

Hobby Horse: 1950

1950/134, Hobby Horse, Cigarette Box, Milk Glass Doe Skin. The Hobby Horse was also produced in Milk Glass Glossy with Hand Painting.

Ski Tumbler: 1950

The Ski Tumbler was first shown in Milk Glass: *Milk Glass Imperial Glass Corporation*, ©2001. It has a translucent look and is different from Imperial's regular milk glass. The design is embossed and hand-painted. According to an Imperial memorandum, when the Ski Tumbler was brought into the market by Imperial, the memorandum instructed the sales staff to market it to the ski resorts. The tumbler definitely does not look like Imperials' familiar milk glass of that period.

#107, Ski Tumbler ©1950s. Instructions on this item was to "promote to the Ski Resorts." $*.

Coach Lamps: 1958-1959

The #460, Coach Lamp Candy Jar can be found with three different designs on Milk Glass. Those designs are Belles of 1890 decorated in Willow Ware Blue color, Pennsylvania Dutch in Olive color, and Gay Nineties in Black. The jar is 6 3/4" tall and 4 5/8" wide and each side has a different design. World known authority, on these arts, Jane Snead (daughter of Imperial's President, Carl Gustkey), designed the Dutch and the Gay Nineties jars. Lynne Pepperdine designed the Belles of 1890. These were available 1958-1959.

#460, Coach Lamp, Olive Pennsylvania Dutch decoration on Milk Glass. $75-100.

#460, Coach Lamp, Crystal, Black trim. $*.

Peach Blow: 1960s

Peachblow is cased glass with a lining of milk glass. The outside is ruby glass that is hearted to turn it ruby and when certain temperatures are met, it will become a light yellow rather than a complete ruby color. Peachblow was made with a glossy as well as a velvet finish.

Six vases were produced. By adding a stopper, two of the vases became decanters. Production was in the 1960s. It was not a very long production life.

There is not a great deal of Peachblow activity to determine prices. The values would range between $100-175 for vases and $200-275 for decanters.

#4038, 10 1/2" Vase (2 bulges rings on neck)
#4038/1, Decanter/stopper (2 bulges)
#4036, 8 3/4" Vase
#4037, 10 1/2" Vase
#980, 7 3/4" Vase (wide base)
#980/1, Decanter (wide base)
#983, 9 1/2" Vase (triangle shape)
#168, 8" Vase

Imperial Photograph. Left, #4036, 8 1/4" Vase; Center, #163, 8" Vase, Right, #4037, 10 1/2" Vase. NP.

#980/1, Decanter. $200-250.

Imperial Photograph. Left, #983, 91/2" Vase; Center #4038, 10 1/2" Vase; Right, #980, 7 3/4" Vase.

Vigna Vetro: 1959

Vigna Vetro definitely comes under the Unique heading. Milk Glass is the basic glass for these. Pieces of glass called "frit" are added to the hot glass for the unusual effect. Blue, Yellow and Green are the colors of the frit. If the frit chips melted completely into the milk glass, they might have been considered slag.

#163 Decanter with Stopper, Grape Design. $90-110;

#180, 7 1/2" Vase. $30-35;

#310, Bud Vase. $30-35;

#241, Cruet with Stopper, Grape. $85-90;

#287, 10" Vase, Grape. $75-90;

#356, 10" Vase, Loganberry. $110-125.

#356, Vigna Vetro.

Murrhina: 1959

Murrhina is the result of an interesting process that results in an unusual finished piece of glass. A "gob" of hot glass is gathered onto a gathering rod that is then rolled in a layer of tiny colored glass particles. The glass is blown some and then rolled in another layer of clear glass. At that time, the article is shaped into the desired piece, which stretches the color particles into various lines and waves—all sizes are approximate-none exact--circa late 1950s.

#591, 11 1/2" Pitcher—Vase
#592, 10 1/4" Pitcher—Vase
#593, 10 1/4" Pitcher—Vase
#594, 10" Pitcher—Vase
#595, 8" Pitcher—Vase
#596, 7 1/2" Pitcher—Vase
#597, 7 1/2" Pitcher—Vase
#598, 7 1/2" Pitcher—Vase
#599, 5 3/4" Pitcher—Vase
#600, 4 3/4" Pitcher—Vase
#601, 4 3/4" Pitcher—Vase
#602, 4 1/4" Pitcher—Vase
#595/1, 8 1/2" Vase
#596/1, 8 1/2" Vase
#597/1, 7 1/2" Vase
#598/1, 7" Vase
#603, 9" Vase
#604, 8" Vase
#605, 8 1/2" Vase
#606, 8 3/4" Vase
#595/2, Bottle and Stopper
#607, 9" Deep Bowl
#608, 9" Shallow Bowl
#609, 8" Shallow Bowl
#610, 6" Handled Nappy

#602, Murrhina Pitcher, 4 1/4". $100-140; #605, 8 1/4" Vase. $130-150.

Whisk Broom: 1960s

#910/1, 7 1/2" Server; Whisk Brooms; (In 1964. five items were made in the Whiskbroom design. They are #611/1, 6" Ftd. Flowerholder; #612, 8" Ftd. Vase; #611, 8" Ftd., Covered Sweetsbowl; #910, 7 1/2" Covered Broom Box;) #910/1, 7 1/2" Server. $20-25.

Roly Poly Tumbler

#785/970, Roly Poly Tumbler, 4 oz. Lunar Dot Cutting, 1953. $5-7.

Decalcomania

#600, 6" Relish and 3" Bowl. Colonial Line. $25-30.

#600, Relish, Mayo Bowl. Colonial. $25-30 each.

#600, Relishes, Matching Ladle. $20-25 each.

Imperial's Iron Cross mark is on this item. In factory-written material is a note indicating that in 1928 Imperial was the first in the American handcrafted glass industry to apply decalcomania transfers to glass. This would be a "decal-like design." (#727 and #728) Three names were on this note; Flora, Orchard, and Phlox; glass items were neatly trimmed with real burnished gold. In 1930 it was discovered that the large quantity of the decals were worthless due to age. They were destroyed at large monetary loss to Imperial Glass Company.

Cape Cod

#160/246, Cape Cod Square Pitcher, Stick Handle 7 oz. The square pitcher had a handle on the side adjacent to the spout. In factory records, there was a notation that the mould was scrapped in 1948. It is not illustrated in any catalog. $*.

Milk Glass

#114763, 9 1/2", Plate, Milk Glass. $20-30. AKA "Heavy Grape" by Carnival Collectors.

Candlewick

#400/36 Canapé Tray; #400/77 AD Cup; Candlewick Gold Canapé Set. $250-300.

Cocktail Pitcher and Tumbler

#142, Cocktail Pitcher, Frosted Band with Stars. $45-50.

Masque Vase

#486, Masque Vase, Smoke Iridescent. $20-30.

Gaffer Vase

#150, Gaffer Vase, no foot, 1953. $15-20.

Smart Alex Tumblers

Occasionally Imperial bought blanks from other companies (Federal Glass Company in this instance) and applied decorations. In the following photo, the witty sayings were sold under the title of "Smart Alec" in 1959. These decorated tumblers were silk screened on blanks. These Tumblers were great icebreakers and were the hit of the party. Each had at least a dozen sayings, e.g., "It is real nice to be important, BUT it's real important to be nice." Is not that true!

#71/Dec. Smart Alex Tumblers; 1959, Federal Glass Blanks. $8-10 each.

Crystal Coil

Crystal Coil, circa 1930s, first group were vases. It is believed that these items followed the vases. A large thread of molten glass was wound around a crystal item such as the #142, a Shaker, Ice Bucket, #871, 12 oz. Tumbler, and #939, Old Fashion with a #701 Reeded Muddler. Not shown were the, #625 Decanter and #812, 2 oz. Whiskey. Imperial factory photograph.

Big Shots

These Imperial photographs show the Big Shot Line better than words can explain.

#711, Big Shots, various sizes can be found. $15-40.

Imperial Photograph

Imperial Photograph

Bird Box

#1950/154, Bird Box. $*.

Fancy Colonial

#582, Fancy Colonial Compote. $35-45.

N I Mark

Perhaps some collectors know that the Show Horse in Amber was made with the NI mark on it. There is also the #106 Miniature Pitcher with the NI. The three items shown in the company photograph were also made with the NI. All of the items will be scarce items. Look carefully for a superimposed NI.

Chapter 9
Art Glass and Freehand: 1920s-1930s

Freehand blown art glass began in 1923 and in 1931 it was dropped. The remaining inventory was sold to the employees. The next several photographs show only a small part of the production of freeform, hand blown Imperial Glass. Some of the photographs were shot at a glass show in a dealer's booth. He enjoyed finding, buying, and displaying them for all to admire and for some to add to their collections. We appreciated the opportunity to photograph them.

We do not have factory information to cover all the shape numbers and color designs. If the color descriptions are our words, they will be in quotation marks.

#199 "Satin Crystal, Turquoise Loops," 2-handles. $750-800; 12/6, #622 Shape, Unknown Color, Possibly "Red Amberina Threaded". $450-525.

#694 Vase, White Ice. $70-85.

#412 Shape, "Marble Blue with White", $250-300; #354, "Pale Peach with Green Chain". $475-550. Possibly #354 without a collar, "Green, Hanging Hearts". $200-250.

#412, "Opal White with Blue Hanging Hearts," $225-275. #412, Lead Lustre "Egg Shell, Olive Loops." $250-300. #655 Shape, "Celery Green, and Almond with Heather Hearts and Vines." $350-450.

#58, 6 1/2" Plate, Pearl Amethyst. $80-100; Vase, from assortment #504, "Rainbow of colors from Green, Yellow, Amethyst," Iron Cross Mark on both. $75-95.

#771, Vase, "Hanging Hearts" 6 1/2", Lead Lustre. "Rainbow of Colors" depending on source of light. $125-175.

#691, Vase, Iridescent Amber Ice. $60-80.

#622/20, Vase, Orange Lead Lustre, 8 3/4" tall $90-100 and #655/20, Orange Lead Lustre, 6 3/4" tall. $75-95.

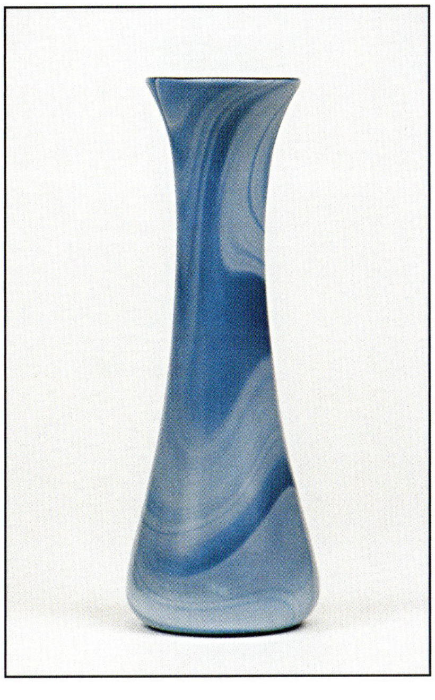

#412, Vase, "Blue Marble." $250-300.

Vase, altered by factory for lamp. These were from the estate of an Imperial Representative. The lamp on the right is assembled with home crafted parts to illustrate the intention of the altered glass vase. Both items had been cut to make a lamp. A few lamps have been found with original light parts. $100-150 each.

Chapter 10
Lamps, Lighting Fixtures and Shades- 1920s to 1940s

Milk Glass

Imperial supplied glass parts to other companies to be adapted for distribution as lamps and light fixtures. Midwest Chandelier, H. A. Framburg, Lightolier, and Imperial Lighting Company (not connected to Imperial Glass Company) were a few of those lighting companies. Many of the distributors remain a mystery to researchers and collectors today.

The photographs of lamps and fixtures are followed by sketches from Imperial's factory records showing glass parts offered to private companies. The sketches, as well as sketches for Irving W. Rice, shown in the book *Imperial's Boudoir, Etcetera...*, have been valuable for assisting in the identification of Imperial designs. Often a light or lamp part incorporates one of Imperial's pattern designs. Candlewick, Cape Cod, "Zippered Heart," Reeded, Laced Edge, Pillar Flute and Washington are among the pattern names found on lighting products.

The sketches may motivate collectors to look for lights, lamps, etc. It is a thrill to spot Imperial glass combined with other materials to make a lighting fixture or lamp. If the distributor of a lamp, etc. is known, it will be given.

1950/425, Covered Compote, Milk Glass, combined with maple wood. Notice that the lid to the covered dish is at the base of the lamp and the container is above that. $50-75.

Lace Edge

#749, Lace Edge Shade. $20-25.

Another illustration of this shade is in the Enchanted Lighting Products Company catalog. The #749 shade is used on a light fixture as a shade, 11 1/2". Shade $20-25. Fixture $75-80.

1950/128, Punch Bowl, on Stand, Grape, Milk Glass. $75-100.

1950/47, Grape Bowl on Stand, Milk Glass. $75-100.

#779, Empire Ceiling fixture with the same glass part as the dresser lamp in following photograph. We cannot find this glass part in company photos or sketches, but when it is compared with an Empire #779 nappy, it is believed to be the same design. $20-25.

1950/103, "Candlewick" Compote (400/103), Milk Glass, combined with metal. $75-100.

#779, Empire Dresser Lamp. Although we are unable to prove this lamp part, we feel that it should be included here to alert collectors to the glass 6" part we think is Imperial's Empire pattern. The same part is on ceiling fixture in the precious photograph. $35-40.

Candlewick

Most of the following lampshades were made for Midwest Chandelier in 1937. This documentation first appeared in *Imperial's Boudoir, Etcetera* © 1996 and later in *Candlewick: Colored and Decorated*, Schiffer Publishing, Ltd., 2003. First, we will show individual shades and then follow with ceiling fixtures using the shades.

#G-109, Candlewick Edge with Raised Flowers Shade, 5/8" hole, and 1 3/4" hole made for Midwest Chandelier, 1941. $85-100

#G-112, Viennese Blue; #G-112 with wire clip to fasten to the bulb, sandblasted; #G-112 Sandblasted and cut, Mid-West Chandelier Company in 1937. $60-70.

#G-107, Shade, sandblasted, three different decorations, with gold trim, with cut, or sandblasted, Mid-West Chandelier Company in 1937. $85-100.

#G-78, Bowl Shade. Midwest Chandelier. $90-110.

#G-78, Bowl Shade, another view, Midwest Chandelier 1937. $90-110.

#G-500, Cut 800, 7 1/2" x 5 1/2" x 3" depth, Midwest Chandelier, 1941. $85-100.

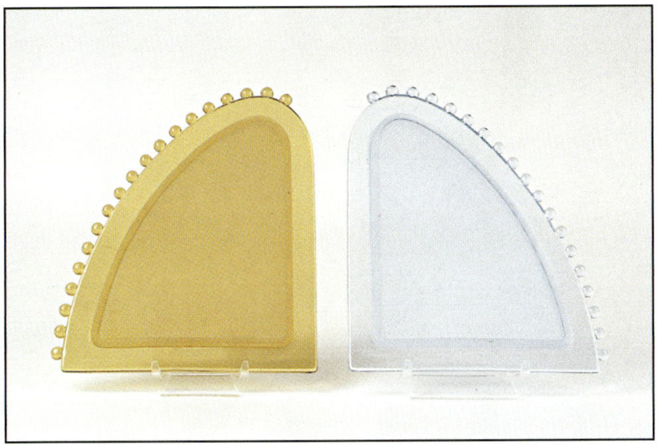

#G-110, Candlewick Panel, Sandblasted both sides, Amber, Blue, (Crystal Frosted, not shown), 7 3/4" x 9", Mid-West Chandelier. $75-90.

#G-110, Candlewick, G-110, the most recent light fixture found. The seller and other friends came to house and hung it—what fun! $*.

The shades are not original to the fixture but experience leads us to believe it is an appropriate match because of design, dates, and lighting company.

G-111, Shade with the 3" base opening. We are unsure of the exact number for this shade; we feel there is no question the shade was made by Imperial Glass. It may be the #108/115 cut for Midwest Chandelier in 1937. It has the same quality and appearance as the G-78, G-107, G-112, and G-500. $85-100.

The shade on the front and back is undocumented, but we feel it is Imperial. It has the typical spacing between beads that the Imperial designed Candlewick has. There is a similar version that has no spacing between beads and we think it is an imposter. We have an Imperial company letter written to another glass company, stating an objection to a conflicting design similar to the design for a shade belonging to Imperial Glass Company. We think the shade shown on left and right might be the discussed conflict. We have no verified information to the maker of either of these shades.

#G-107, Shade, Sand/blast outside, gray cutting; original fixture, Mid-West Chandelier. $700-800.

Front and Back shades we believe are Imperial but they are not documented. We believe that the shades on the left and right are imposters. $45-55. Imposters. $5-10.

#G-107, Sandblast outside, gold print and bands, original fixture, the Cream Paint on part of fixture is original and was often used on other fixtures. Mid-West Chandelier. $750.-850.

This fixture is original condition. The shade has the ivory finish of the imposters but it had the bead size and spacing of the ones we feel are Imperial. Please remember that we cannot document these shades. $50-75.

#G-78, Round Shade, 6", Amber or Crystal with cut or gold print design. Fixture was refurbished, polished, and brushed brass; originally, we believe it had white or cream finish painted by the fixture company. $900-1000.

#G-107, original fixture, Candlewick Ceiling Fixture, Sandblasted with gold trim on edge and medallion, Mid-West Chandelier. $750-800.

#G-107 Den, Sconce matches the preceding ceiling fixture, original fixture, Mid-West Chandelier. $200-225.

#G-790 AKA #400/155, Candlewick Floor Lamp; part made for Lightolier Lamp Company, all original. $250-300.

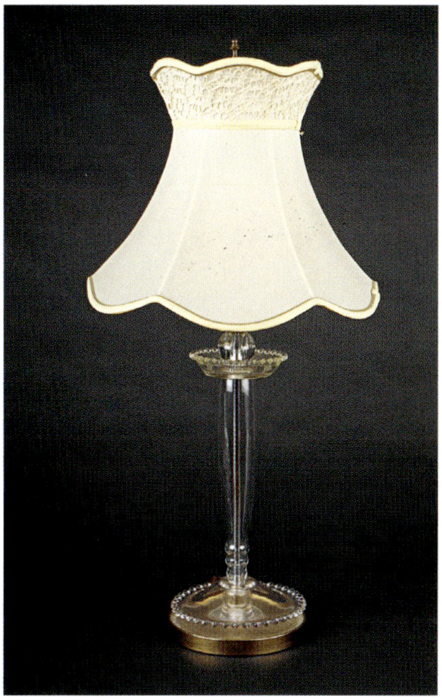

Candlewick Table Lamp #400/33 Individual Jelly; #400/86 Mushroom Candleholder; #451 Bud Vase, foot cut off; Nelson Bead Company, 1941, all original. $275-300.

Candlewick Table Lamp; #400/33 Jelly, #400/86 Mushroom Candleholder, Glass Cylinder, all original. $250-275.

#G-790 AKA #400/155, made for Lightolier. $175-200.

Boudoir, Lamp Candlewick, #400/400 Ash Tray, inverted, 3" glass ball, and glass rod, several pairs known to exist, original. $180-200.

#G-790, AKA Lightolier #155 part made by Imperial, generic shade. We have seen the #155 part put with many different shades for ceiling light fixtures, original fixture. $200-225.

Two views of another Lightolier #155. We were told that the fixture was all original. $175-200.

Cape Cod

For twenty-two years we have watched for any distributor names of the lamps pictured below. These lamps were first shown in *Imperial Cape Cod Tradition to Treasure*© 1982, *Imperial's Boudoir, Etcetera* ©1996 and then again in *Imperial Cape Cod* © 2005, Schiffer Publishing, Ltd. We have not found the wanted information and we hope that showing them here again may bring some information.

#160/163, Cape Cod Decanter inverted all original, unknown distributor. $150-175.

#160/163, Cape Cod Decanter inverted with stopper on top. All original; unknown distributor. $175-200.

Cape Cod Boudoir Lamp, 160/134 Individual Butter, #160/133 Individual Jelly and Glass Rod, original; We know of two other pairs of this lamp, therefore, we can assume they are original, unknown distributor. $150-175.

#160/143, Flip Vase, 8 1/2"; there is no foot on the vase, there is an extra plain glass base, all original; unknown distributor. $175-200.

Other Styles

#699, Washington Compote light. $100-125.

#201, AKA Zipper Loop; This is the way the new owner bought this. We are showing it in case others have found similar. It could have been homemade or it could have been made by an after factory distributor. The age and condition of the metal and the way it is assembled appear to be a professional item. $100-125.

#474 Lamp Shade. $45-50.

#474 Lamp Shade for a side view.

#743, Grape Shade, Crystal Satin, has the same design that Imperial used with a luncheon set and many other grape items in milk glass. $30-40.

#975, Candy Jar, Decorated Cranberry. It was exciting to have this fixture pointed out to us by our granddaughter who admires cranberry decorated articles. At that time, she did not know that Imperial made this glass part, which was transformed into a ceiling fixture. We have found another one that has an amber stain on the raised teardrop; a theory of a fellow collector is this—if you find an after factory item in different areas, you know it is not likely a "home made article". Unknown decorator and distributor. $75-85.

#975, Candy Jar, Marigold Iridescent Stain. Remember, two items found in different parts of the country help a collector and researcher to think that the items are not homemade. This is not a complete fixture. It is missing the prisms with wires. $25-30.

Chapter 11
Animals and Figurals

Imperial glass figural shapes are seldom seen; the examples shown are part of a large private glass animal collection. Several are in crack-off, unpublished, or undocumented colors. We appreciate the opportunity to include them and share his information.

Owl, Amber. $40-60; Owl, Sunshine Yellow. $40-60.

Story Book Mug Creamer, Whimsy. $150-200.

Donkey on Bust-off, Milk Glass; Glossy, IG Mark, Frosted, IG Mark. $400-500.

Owl, Blue Opaque Milk Glass, marked ALIG.$ 25-50.

Donkey, Meadow Green; (this one has the #57 on it), marked LIG. $350-400.

Dumbo Elephant Mugs are a group that were a special order for E. Ward Russell for various Republican functions.

Amber Mug, 1968, Lincoln Day Dinner; not marked EWR. $100-125.

Opalescence Moonstone (Green) 1974, Ford-Rockerfellow, marked EWR $125-150. (Westmoreland Glass Company product using the privately owned mould.)

Antique Blue 1969, Nixon Agnew, marked EWR, IG. $40-60.

Azalea 1970, Spiro Agnew, marked EWR, IG. $40-60.

Blue Haze 1973, Nixon-Agnew, marked EWR, IG. $40-60.

Plum 1973 EWR Nixon-Ford, marked EWR. $40-60.

Light Green 1968, GOP Women's Conference. $100-125.

Dumbo Elephant Mugs.

Hen, Crack off, Milk Glass carnival, IG Mark. $250. (Three made according to one authority) Scratched or needle marked on bust-off was REC 1-15-79; PMH 1-15-79; JWH 1-16-79; BZ 2-10-79; On three labels on the bust off were these words; purchased from Michael Penyak 1-15-79; (signed) Richard E Collins. Purchased from, 1-15-79 Patricia M Hogue; Received from Richard E Collins and Patricia M. Hogue 1-16-79, (signed) James W Haddix.

Head Down Chick, Crack off, IG Mark $70-80; Bunny, Head Up, Medium, IG Mark. $70-80. Bunny Head Up, Small, IG Mark. $70-80.

Duck, Milk Glass $500-600.

Cygnet, Frosted Pink. $150-175.

Hen, Frosted Pink, IG Mark. $250-300.

Horse, Head Back, Green. $250-300.

Horse, Head Back, Close Up, another view. $250-300.

Duck, Ultra Blue Carnival. $250-300.

Parlor Pup, Crack Off, Yellow $75-100.

Parlor Pup, Ear Down, on Crack Off, Amethyst Carnival. $70-90.

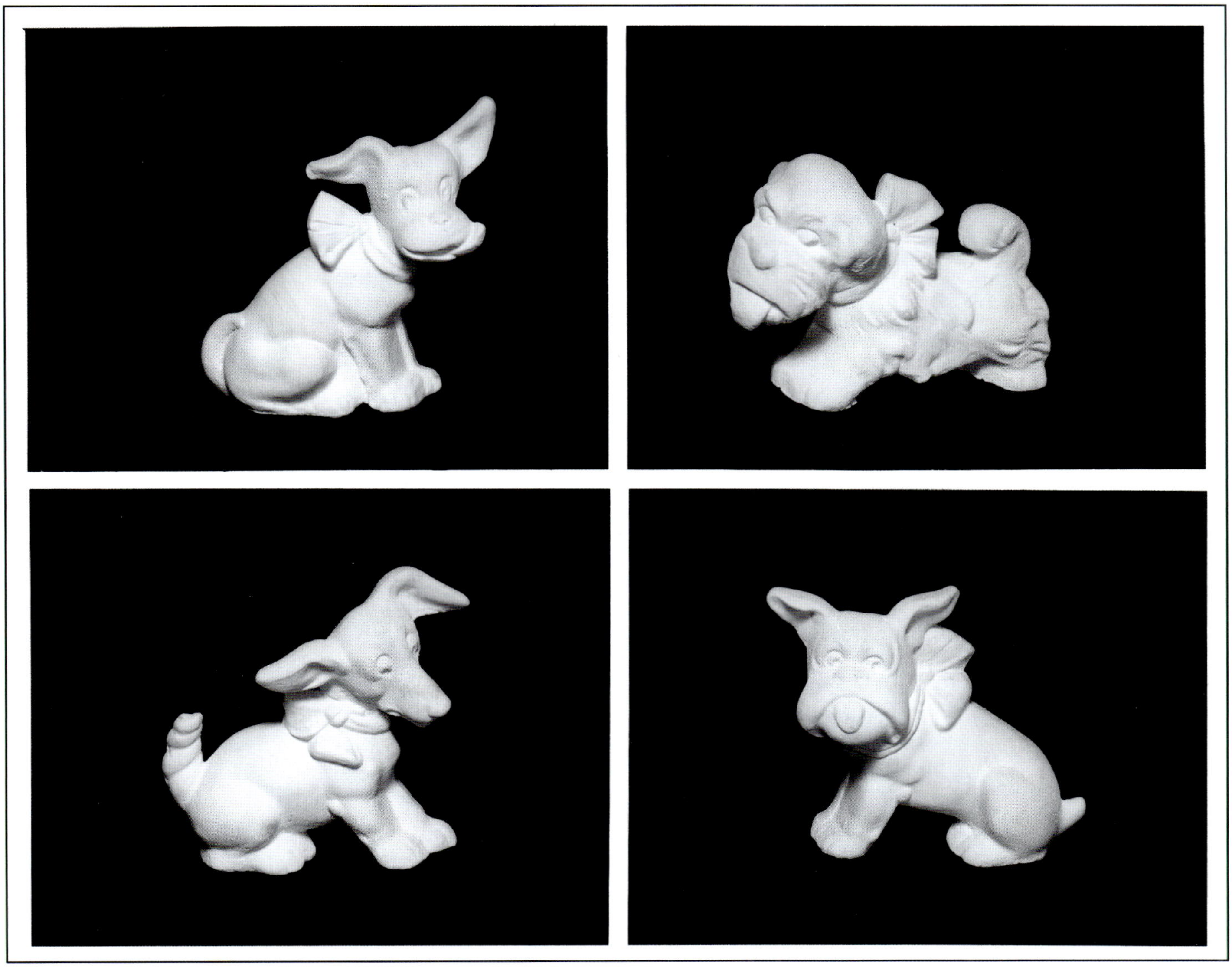

Imperial Photograph of the Parlor Pups.

Rearing Horse, Black Satin. $650-750.

Hen, Charcoal, Frosted. $325-375.

Pig, Amber. $400-450; Horse, Chest Out, Amber. $225-275.

Rabbit, Yellow. $400-450.

Egret, Cranberry, Frosted, Glossy. $400-450.

Elephants, front, Pink $100; middle, Pink Frosted $70; back, Pink Carnival. $70. All have LIG and ALIG Mark.

Elephant, Medium, left. $600-650; Elephant, Small, right, Milk Glass. $350-450.

Elephant, Pale Pink. $150-250.

Elephant, Small, Meadow Green, Marked LIG or ALIG. $120-140.

Head Down Bunny, ALIG Mark, Nut Brown $80-90.

Show Horse, Amber, NI Mark. This was the mark for New Imperial during the time it was hoped the company could be saved. There were only a few items made with the NI mark. $1000-$1200.

Horse Handle Mug. Proto Type. $*.

Reproductions

Eagles Blue Base, $250 Set. Eagle Amber Base, Made by Fenton for the National Imperial Glass Collectors' fund raiser. The Blue Base was chosen and the Amber was made for the club to have a choice of color. $*

Proto type of Horse Mug; Written on this item are there words, "This piece push out from the back." An arrow points to upper and lower holes. $*.

Chapter 12
Private Mould Customers

Imperial Glass Company had other avenues of selling its products besides the representatives and showrooms that sold Imperial products to retail consumers. The following discussion of companies gives a brief glimpse of some of Imperial's customers. All the dates given are from a limited source of company papers. At the time of Imperial's liquidation, many written records were lost. It is not known how long the relationships lasted.

Although the Imperial Glass Corporation had many "private mould customers," only a short, incomplete list from the 1930s to 1940s is available to share with collectors. Even this partial list can be valuable if more information is found. There were other line numbers mentioned in company records, but not sufficient information to be included here. Although this section has only a few illustrations, the facts may help to identify items made for Imperial's private mould customers, customers who sold the patterns, and whether an item is original, an after-factory item, or homemade. Also, it may aid future research into merchandising.

The chapter is divided into the following six groups:

I. Glass made from customers' moulds or moulds specially made by Imperial for customers

II. Glass made from Imperial's moulds for customers to alter before selling

III. Glass made for customers to decorate and sell as own product

IV. Glass made from Imperial's moulds for customers to market as its own product

V. Glass made from Imperial's moulds in special colors or decorations for customers

VI. Glass made for customers' business use

I.

Glass Made From Customers' Moulds or Moulds Specially Made by Imperial for Customers

Metropolitan Museum of Art
Smithsonian Institution
Irving W. Rice Company
A. Harris Company
Crown Silver Company
Monmouth Silver Company
Lightolier Lighting
Midwest Chandelier Company
PeeGee Company
E. Ward Russell
Telephone Pioneers of America
West Virginia Centennial
Jamestowne Village
Cathedral Art Metal Company
Chaplains Aid Association
International Silver Company
H.A. Framburg Company

Imperial Glass Corporation had the distinction of producing glass items for the Metropolitan Museum of Art (MMA) of New York City and the Smithsonian Institution (SI) of Washington, D.C. to sell in their gift shops. Later, Imperial had the right to offer some of these items for sale through its own catalogs. All items bear the marks SI or MMA.

Metropolitan Museum of Art, New York City: circa 1968-1977

The Metropolitan Museum of Art (MMA) commissioned Imperial Glass Corporation to reproduce several of the glass artifacts on display in the museum. MMA made models of the objects and Imperial chipped the moulds to be used. MMA did not risk relinquishing possession of the museum pieces. The reproductions were marked with raised letters "MMA," to distinguish them from the original items. Most of the reproduction items were made in Crystal, only a few were made in other colors as noted on the following list. From 1977-1983, Imperial had the right to sell these items through its own gift shop. The following MMA items are listed in the Imperial catalogs.

#71064, 3 1/2" Diamond & Sunburst Tumbler
#71069, Barrel Tumbler, 4-pc. set in Crystal and Amber
#71071, Ashburton Tumbler, 4-pc. Set
#71155, 4 1/4" Diamond & Sunburst Pitcher, Ruby, Emerald Green, Canary Yellow, Amber
#71180, 10 1/2" Magnet & Grape Covered Jar
#71180, 10 1/2" Diamond & Sunburst Decanter & Stopper
#71241, Diamond & Sunburst Cordial, 4-pc. set
#71371, Plate, 6 1/4" 4-pc. set
#71406, 8" Plate, 4-pc. set
#71530, 8 1/2" Magnet & Grape Covered Jar
#71540, Pitcher
#71571, 6 1/4" Nappy, 4-pc. set
#71590, 8" Oval Lacy Relish Tray
#71661, Salt Trencher, Sky Blue, Emerald Green, Canary Yellow
#71695, 10 1/2" Halley's Comet Bowl
#71712, 3" Diamond & Sunburst Hat
#71755, 6" Quilted Diamond Flip, Vase

#71757, 26 oz. Bellflower Pitcher
#71758, 27 oz. 6 1/4" Diamond & Sunburst Pitcher
#71758, 6 1/4" Plate 4-pc. set
#71762, 10 1/2" Dolphin Candlestick, Sapphire, Emerald Green

Flower Pot and Saucer, Milk Glass. $20-25.

Flower Pot and Saucer, Opaque Blue. $25-30.

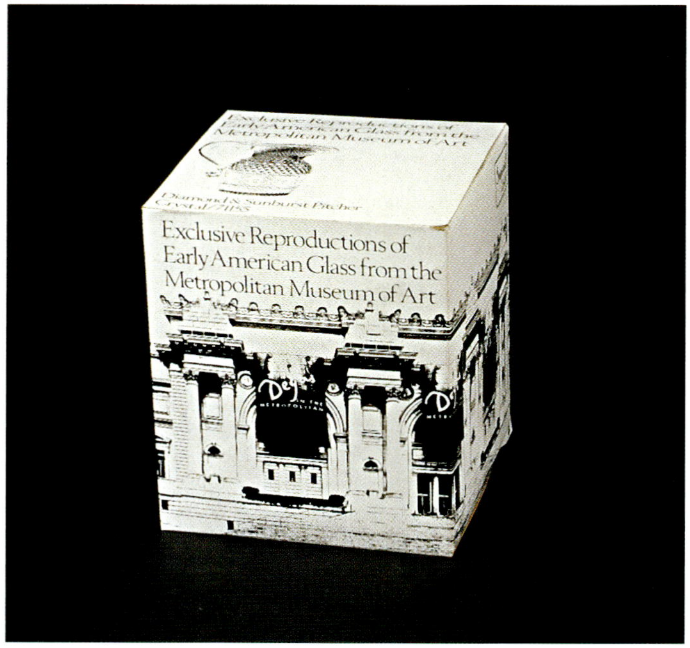

Gift box for the items purchased in the Metropolitan Museum Gift Shop. $5-8.

Smithsonian Institution, Washington, D.C.: 1977-1980

Imperial Glass Corporation was chosen to produce glass for the Smithsonian Institution gift shop. So that these reproductions would never be confused with the originals, every item was marked with raised letters "SI." Imperial was allowed to sell these items through its own catalogs.
#71690, 8" Bowl, 1978-1980
#71790, 5 1/2" Handled Candleholder, 1977-1980

#71251, 4-pc. Wine/Cordial Set, 1977-1980
#71977S, 4 1/2" x 2 3/4" Angel Paperweight, 1980
#71545, 5 1/2" Broken Column Covered Sugar, 1979-1980
#71544, 4 1/4" Broken Column Creamer, 1979-1980
#71360, 6 1/4" ABC Plate, 1977-1980
#71380, 8" Broken Column Server, 1979-1980
#71561, 2-pc. 4 5/8" Broken Column Nappy, 1978-1980

#71750, 4 1/2" Broken Column Spoon holder/Vase, 1978-1980
#71794, 7 3/4" Candlestick, 1980
#71165, 9" Broken Column Pitcher, 1980
#71055, 3 3/4" ABC Tumbler, 1980

#71545 Sugar and #71544 Cream, Broken Column. $30-40 set.

#71165 Large Pitcher; $25-35; #71544 Small Pitcher, Broken Column. $15-20.

#71360, ABC, 6 1/2" Plate. $15-20.

#71794, Candleholder, Stick, Ultra Blue, 1980. $20-25.

Irving W. Rice Company: 1940s-1950s

The Irving W. Rice Company (Irice) was probably Imperial's largest private mould customer. Irice was a distributor of dresser and table top items. When Irice could no longer purchase glass perfume and cologne bottles from Czechoslovakia, due to the outbreak of World War II, they turned to Imperial to make these items during the 1940s and 1950s.

The complete story of the bottles and boxes made for Irice is thoroughly discussed in our book, *Imperial's Boudoir, Etcetera... A brief look at Irving W. Rice Company*. More than 800 cards in the Imperial card file relate to business with this company. Over 400 of the cards have sketches of the items, and most include the dates and quantities of items manufactured. The sketches were made by Carl J. Uhrmann, who served as Imperial's president from 1967 until 1973. Today items matching the sketches are found although no information of production appeared on the card for that item.

Some items had pressed designs and others had cut, acid-etched or hand-painted designs. Gold trim was another decoration applied by the company decorators. Crystal was the major color, while pink and blue glass captured some of the market.

The Czechoslovakian bottles and powder boxes had designs cut into the glass. Irice asked Imperial to place the designs in the moulds and press the wares. Pressing the designs in the mould was less costly than to hand-cut an item.

A. Harris Company, Dallas, Texas: 1936

Imperial made glass for the Texas Centennial in 1936. Using specially made moulds by Imperial Glass, several items were produced for A. Harris Company, Dallas, Texas. These were made in 1936 commemorating 100th Anniversary of Texas Independence in 1836. A. Harris planned to have another group made every ten years to commemorate the independence. The second group, made in dark blue was issued in 1946, but when it failed to be profitable, the plan for a reissue every ten years was dropped. It is not known if all original items were reissued in 1946, but the original 1936 group made in Crystal included:

8" Plate
3 ½" Sherbet
3" Coaster or Ash Tray
9" Pitcher, 1/2 Gallon
6" Goblet
4 1/2" Tumbler, 10 oz.
11 3/4" Platter
Salt and Pepper
Cigarette Box
Lone Star Paperweight

In 1953, Imperial made three CW peg nappies in Forest Green Color #67 which is a medium green. A peg nappy has a threaded peg on the underneath side to be screwed into a silver or brass candleholder base. These items in Forest Green are very rare.

#400/240 7" Plate

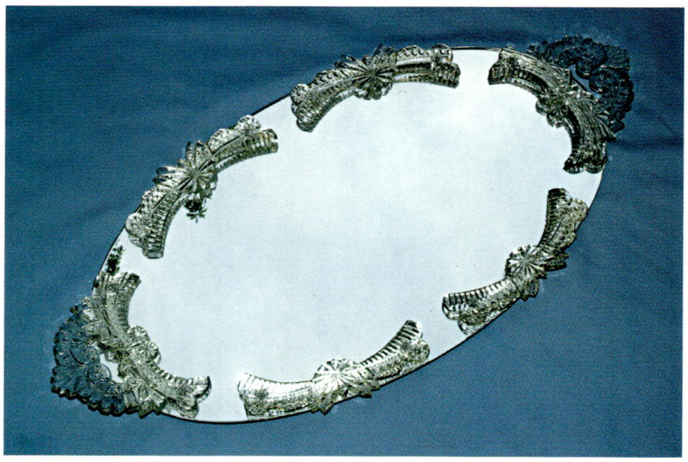

#R-792 End Handles and R-793 Side Handles, Zippered Heart Tray. The dresser tray with one side handle on each side was made for Irice. It is unknown if this set with the two side handles was also made for Irice. $*

8" Plate 1836-1936, (1936 Edition); 8" Plate 1836-1936, (1946 Edition) 3" Coaster or Ash Tray, (1936 Edition). $30-40 each.

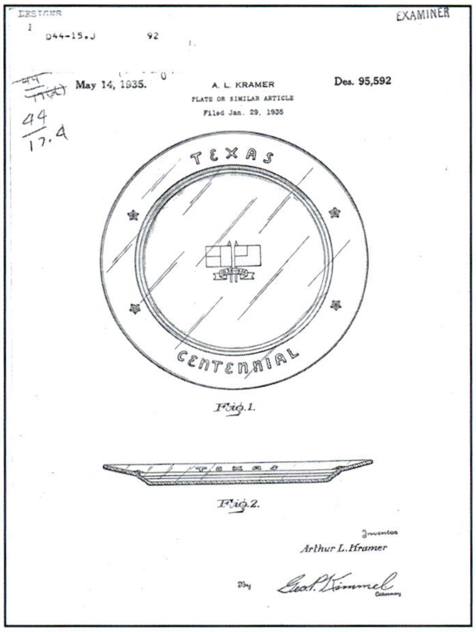

Texas Centennial Patent Application. Design by A.L. Kramer.

Crown Silver Company: 1950s and 1960s

Crown Silver Company was a Private Mould Customer with Imperial during the 1950s and 1960s. Several items in Candlewick were done for Crown Silver. Information about this can be found in *Candlewick: Colored and Decorated,* by Myrna and Bob Garrison, Schiffer Publishing, Ltd., 2003.

#400/240F 6" Nappy
#400/240B 5 3/4" Bowl

The following item was the first that we have known about in the color Forest Green. Fortunately, we had found paper reference to this item #400/240 Plate being made in Forest Green for Crown Silver Company. Upon finding this piece, a friend turned to our book on *Candlewick: Color and Decorated*, to see if there was a reference to this. From the brief mention of a green item being made for Crown Silver, she decided to take a chance on it. Her find sent us back to catalogs and we found a few illustrations of items in Forest Green that led us to know that the Candlewick green piece was indeed Forest Green.

#400/240, 7" Plate, Forest Green. $*.

Later, this same collector happened upon a pair of 400/240F Peg Nappies on an auction site. Today, each of us has one of the 400/240F Peg Nappies. This is a prime example why we believe that sharing something as simple as a list might lead to a rare find and documentation.

Monmouth: 1970

Imperial made two items for Monmouth. The peg items were to be combined with a sterling base.

#400/251X, 10" Peg Bowl
#400/251D, 12" Peg Plate (company information label was on this piece when we bought it)

Lightolier Company: 1940s

Lighting parts for different companies were a large business for Imperial. One of their largest accounts was Lightolier Company. We were fortunate to have access to copies of factory pages showing sketches of glass parts that were made especially for Lightolier. The records date from 1939-1941.

To help collectors identify lighting fixtures and lamps, these sketches of glass parts that Imperial made for Lightolier Lighting Company in the 1940s are presented in the same outline form as they appeared in company papers. When you see numbers preceded by the # sign, we believe these are pattern or item numbers. We leave it up to the collector to match these numbers with information in this and other Imperial books. We do not want to take away the fun of putting this puzzle together. In Chapter 10, Lighting Fixtures and Shades, examples are shown. These sketches will be of value to collectors who share interest in the Imperial Glass Company or lighting fixtures. The sketches will certainly cause collectors to be looking upward. It is exciting when you spot a fixture with one of these parts; we have done it fifty-two times.

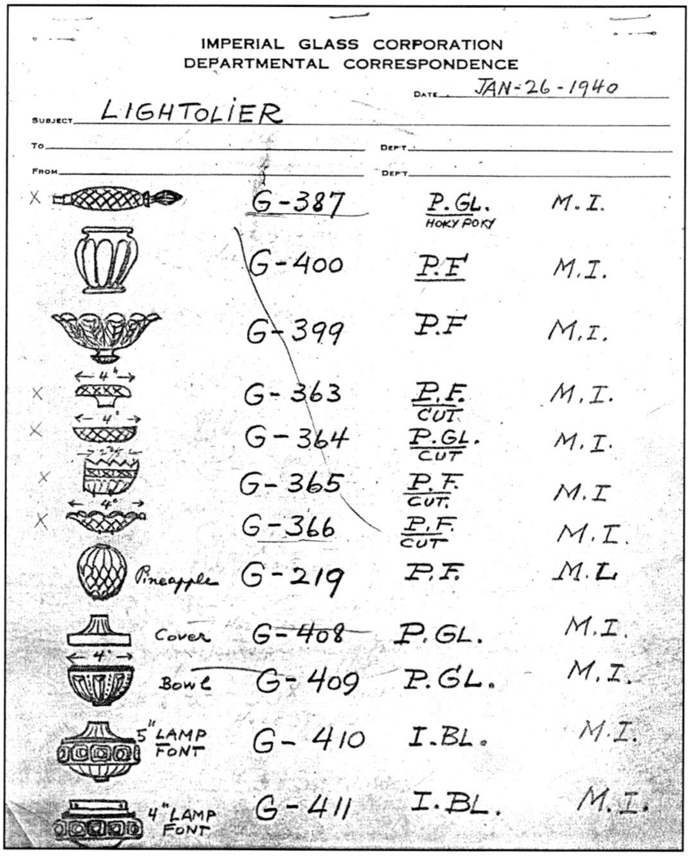

IMPERIAL GLASS CORPORATION
DEPARTMENTAL CORRESPONDENCE

DATE JAN-26-1940

SUBJECT LIGHTOLIER

TO — DEPT.

FROM — DEPT.

G-387	P.GL. HOKY POKY	M.I.
G-400	P.F.	M.I.
G-399	P.F	M.I.
G-363	P.F. CUT	M.I.
G-364	P.GL. CUT	M.I.
G-365	P.F. CUT.	M.I
G-366	P.F. CUT	M.I.
Pineapple G-219	P.F.	M.I.
Cover G-408	P.GL.	M.I.
Bowl G-409	P.GL.	M.I.
5" LAMP FONT G-410	I.BL.	M.I.
4" LAMP FONT G-411	I.BL.	M.I.

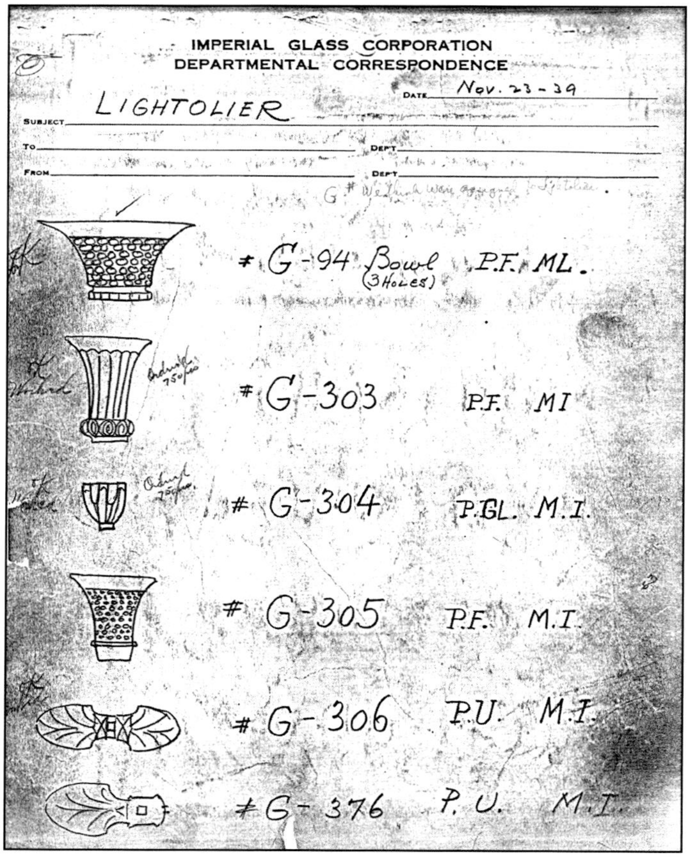

IMPERIAL GLASS CORPORATION
DEPARTMENTAL CORRESPONDENCE

DATE Nov. 23-39

SUBJECT LIGHTOLIER

TO — DEPT.

FROM — DEPT.

#G-94 Bowl (3 HOLES)	P.F.	M.I.
#G-303	P.F.	MI
#G-304	P.GL.	M.I.
#G-305	P.F.	M.I.
#G-306	P.U.	M.I.
#G-376	P.U.	M.I.

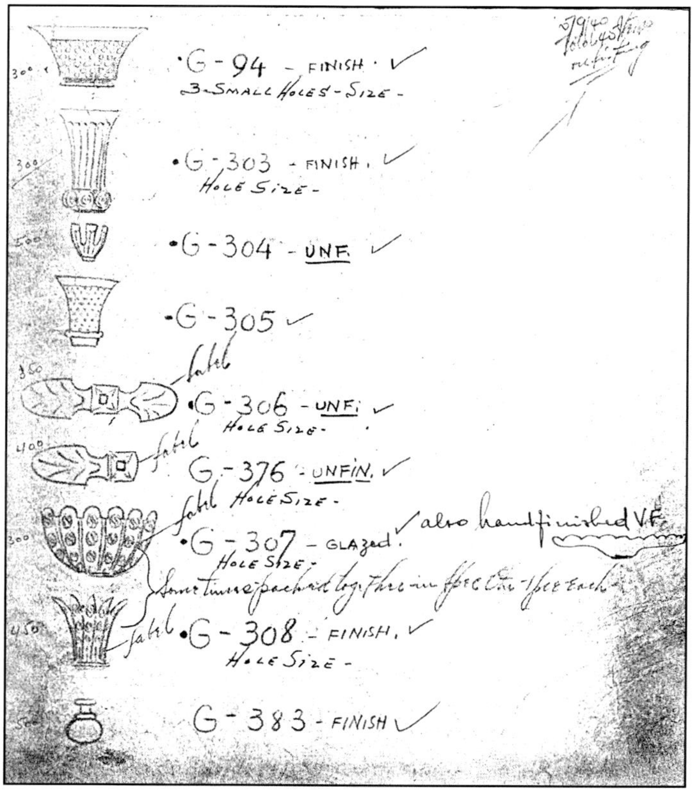

G-94 - FINISH ✓
3-SMALL HOLES-SIZE-

G-303 - FINISH ✓
HOLE SIZE-

G-304 - UNF. ✓

G-305 ✓

G-306 - UNF. ✓
HOLE SIZE-

G-376 - UNFIN. ✓
HOLE SIZE-

G-307 - GLAZED ✓ also hand finished V.F.
HOLE SIZE-

G-308 - FINISH ✓
HOLE SIZE-

G-383 - FINISH ✓

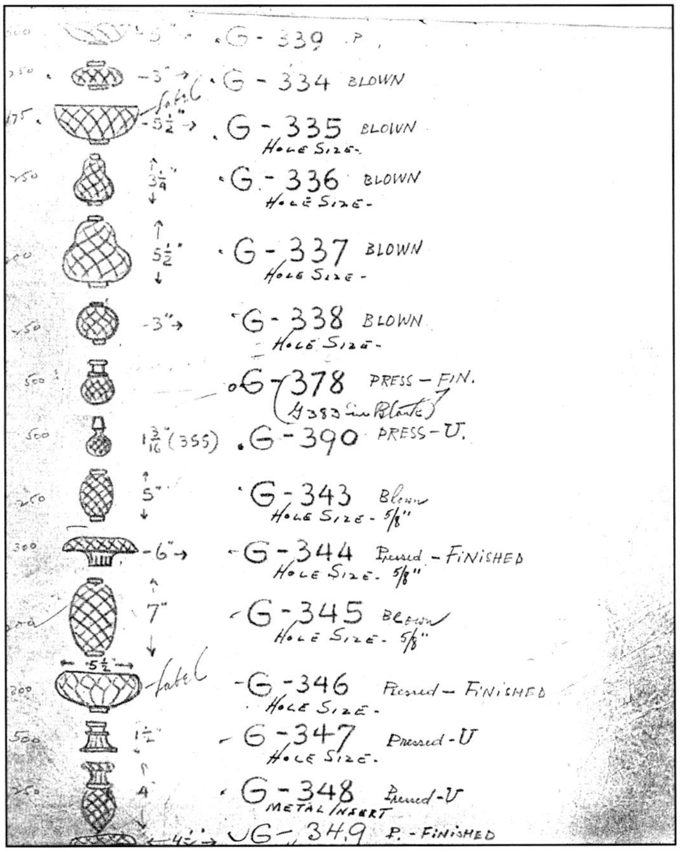

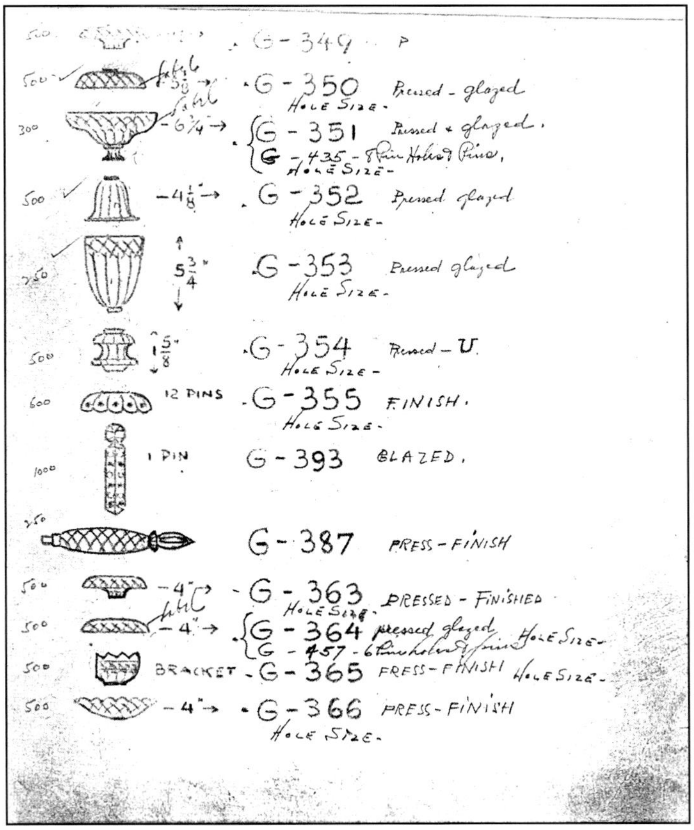

Sketches of parts for Lightolier Light Company.

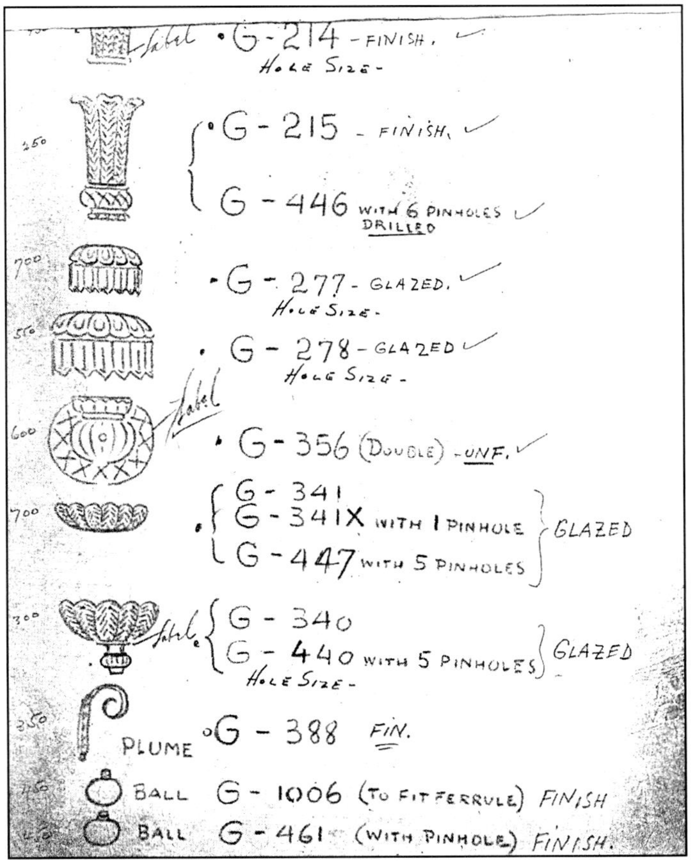

G-94, Basket With 3 Holes
G-214, Omit Customer's Labels
G-215, Holes
G-219, Pineapple
G-233, Decorated
G-258, 16" Bowl, Decorated
G-277
G-278, Omit Customer's Labels
G-303
G-304
G-305
G-306, Frosted , Clear Center
G-307
G-308, Packed With G-307 (#925/B)
G-334/Cut, 3" Oval Ball
G-355/Cut, 5 1/2" Bowl
G-336/Cut, 3 1/4" Spindle
G-337/Cut, 5 1/2" Spindle
G-338/Cut, 3" Ball
G-339/Cut, 5" Bobeche
G-341, Fire Polished
G-340
G-343/Cut, 5"
G-344, 6", 8 Pin Holes and Pins
G-345/Cut, 7"
G-346/Cut, 5 1/2"
G-347/Cut, 1 1/2"
G-348/Cut, 4" Metal Inserted Screw
G-349/Cut, 4 1/2", 6 Pin Holes and Pins
G-350/Cut, 5 1/8"
G-351/Cut, 6 3/4", Holes
G-352/Cut, 4 1/8"

G-353/Cut, 5 3/4"
G-354/Cut, 1 5/8"
G-355, Cut, Bobeche, 12 Mitres, 12 Stars, 12 Holes and Pins, Acid Polished
G-356, Fire Polished
G-363-A/Cut, 4"
G-363/Cut, 4", 5 In Holes and Pins
G-364/Cut, 4" Bracket, Holes
G-365/Cut, Bracket
G-366/Cut, 4" Bobeche
G-368
G-376, Frosted-Clear Center, #930/3
G-376B, Frosted
G-378/Cut, Finial
G-383 (G-854 "New") (We Have Found This Finial On Some Of Our Light Fixtures.)
G-387, Spike
G-388, Plume, L Shape (End To Fit Their Ferrule (#682)
G-390, 1 3/16" Ball
G-393, 1 Pin, Colonial Star Prism With Pins Inserted
G-399, #932/3 [Upside Down Lid]
G-400, Crystal, Ruby, Blue, and Gold Decorated
G-408, 4" Crystal, Ruby
G-409, 4", Crystal, Ruby
G-410, 5", Crystal, Blue Or Champagne Or Ruby.
G-411, 4" Lamp Font, Crystal, Blue Or Champagne, Or Ruby
G-435/Cut, Same As G-351 But With 8 Pin Holes and Pins
G-437, 1 1/8" Hole In Bottom
G-440, Same As G-340 But With 5 Pinholes
G-438, Gray Flutes, Clear Lines
G-446, Same As G-215 But With 6 Pin Holes
G-439, Gray Flutes, Clear Lines
G-447, Same As G341 But With 5 Pinholes
G-461, Ball, (Same As G-1006 But With Pinhole)
G-459, Fire Polished
G-468, Same As G-411 But Ruby
G-470, 4 1/2" Top and 2" Base
G-472, 12" Bowl, Decorated (Their #972-4)
G-474, 4 3/4", Crystal, Blue, Ruby, Decorated Gold, Crystal Decorated Gold.
G-497, 5" Shade, Decorated
G-498, 4"
G-507, 5 1/2", Shade, Decorated #984/3
G-509, Part, Decorated #989/3
G-508, 12" Bowl, Decorated, #981/3
G-510, 10" Bowl, Decorated #979/1
G-511, 8", Bowl, Decorated, #973/6
G-514, Reflector, Decorated Colored Enamels
G-514-A, Reflector, #994/3
G-520, 6" Bowl, Decorated, #977/1
G-521, Part, Decorated, #990/3
G-535, 16" Bow, Decorated, #974/4
G-536, 6", Spindle
G-545,12" Bowl, Decorated
G-546, 12", Decorated
G-547, 3-Part Unit, Decorated
G-562, 14" Bowl, Sandblasted
G-575, Part, Sandblast Inside
G-576, Part Sandblast Inside
G-563, 15" Part, Large Hole, Sandblasted
G-563-A, 15" Part Small Hold, Lalique
G-564, 13" Bowl, Decorated
G-577, Part, Decorated, Gray Floral Cutting, 3 Holes Drilled.
G-586, 5" Clear Bobeche, Crimped Edge and 1 1/8" Hole In Center
G-596, 1 1/8" Pendant Ball With Pins
G-597, Lily Bowl, 7/16" Hole In Bottom, #3305N (We Will Give You A Hint--#330 Is "Diamond Block.")
G-610, Sandblasts Panels
G-626/Cut, 2" Pear-Shaped Pendent
G-631, 1 1/8" Ball
G-634, Part, Crystal, Gray Cutting, 6 Pin Holed and Pins Polished Cutting
G-637/Cut, 4" Bobeche, Gray Cutting
G-642/Cut, Part Polished Cutting
G-643/Cut, Part, Gray Cutting
G-643/Cut, 5" Part Gray Cutting
G-645/Cut, 4 1/2" Part Polished Cutting
G-646/Cut, 6" Part, Polished Cutting
G-652/Cut, 1 3/4" Ball, Polished Cutting
G-657, Part
G-662/Cut, 13" Chimney Part, Gray Cutting, Must Fit G-664; (Same Blue/Ruby Stain)
G-664, 3 1/2" Base Crystal Plain Or Lalique
G-666/Cut, 10" Chimney Part, Crystal, Gray Cutting, Frosted, (Same Blue/Ruby Stain)
G-667/Cut, 9" Chimney Part, Crystal, Gray Cutting, Frosted Band, (Same Blue Stain)
G-668/Cut, 10" Chimney Part, Crystal, Gray Cutting, Frosted Band (Same Blue/Gold-Ruby Stain)
G-669/Cut, 6" Base Crystal Part, Gray Cut Punties (Same Blue/Gold-Ruby Stain)
G-670/Cut, 11" Chimney Crystal Part, Gray Cutting, Frosted Band (Same Gold-Ruby Stain)
G-673, Base (Their Mould)
G-658/Cut, 12" Bowl, Decorated
G-669/Cut, 14" Bowl, Decorated
G-665
G676, Part, Crystal, Frosted, Clear Beads, Slots In Bottom
G-677, 10" Part Sandblasted, Clear Frosting
G-678, 5" Part, Etched Clear Frosting 1/2" Hole [Looks Like The Eagle Holder To Us]
G-681, Lightolier Ash Tray, Gray Glass, Intaglio Frosted Bottom
G-690/Cut, 13" Bowl
G-694, 5" Part, Decorated
G-695, 6" Part, Decorated [Reeded #701?]
G-701, Part Plain
G-702, Part Lalique Finish Only
G-703, Part, Decorated
G-749, 9 1/2"
G-750, 5 1/4" Part
G-790, Part
G-791, Finial (X-8 Stopper)
G-792, Finial (400/70 Stopper)
G-794, Reflector, Decorated Pink Enamel (Same As G-514)
G-795, Reflector, Decorated Blue Enamel (Same As G-514)
G-826, 12"
G-827, 15"
G-923/Cut Finial, Clear and Gray Cutting (E-121)
G-924/Cut, Finial, Frosted and Clear Cutting (E-121)
G-925/Cut, Finial Ruby Stained and Gray Cut, Fluted (E-121)
G-926/Cut, Finial, White Enamel, Fluted and Polished (E-121)

Midwest Chandelier Company: 1937

Another lighting manufacturer that was a large customer of Imperial's was Midwest Chandelier Company, in 1937. Collectors have found several different styles of chandeliers and sconces. This company is also discussed and illustrated in *Candlewick: Colored and Decorated*. Refer to the Lamps, Lighting Fixtures, and Shades section for examples.

PeeGee Company: 1981

PeeGee Glass Company was one of Imperial's Private Mould Customers and would probably rank among the least known of Imperial's Private Mould Customers. The Mouse Lovers began in 1981 and were made for a couple in Ft. Wayne, Indiana.

The idea for the Pee Gee Mouse Lovers originated from a ceramic animal figure of standing mice. A mould was designed to have the mice sitting. Imperial was contacted about making the mice for the PeeGee Glass Company. The pieces are marked with a P superposed over a G and 81 for the year on the back. Production was limited to 1000 pieces. All items were to be marked with ALIG and a different color was to be made each month. The items were produced just before Imperial went into bankruptcy in 1982. After the closing of Imperial, Pee Gee turned to Viking to make the Mouse Lovers. The marks are faint. Exactly what colors were made by Imperial is unknown to us, but we do know these were made; Milk Glass, Pink, Sunshine Yellow, Sunshine Yellow with hand painting, Caramel Slag with hand painting, Nut Brown, and Cobalt Frosted with hand-painting.

A neat group of the Pee Gee Mouse Lovers from a private collection. $25-60.

Pee Gee Mouse Lover in Ultra Blue, Hand Painted $40.

Pee Gee Mouse Lover in Caramel Slag, Hand Painted $60.

Pee Gee Mouse Lover in Amethyst Carnival $50.

E. Ward Russell: 1960s-1970s

E. Ward Russell, of Maryland, was a staunch supporter of the Republican party. He had special orders for Dumbo Mugs made as well as American the Beautiful plates in Carnival colors (see Dumbo Mugs on page 143.

Telephone Pioneers of America: 1960s

Telephone Pioneers of America, 1911 to present, was an interesting Imperial private mould customer. The purpose of this organization is "to promote and participate in activities that respond to community needs and problems, to provide a means of friendly association for eligible telecommunication employees and a spirit of mutual helpfulness, to contribute to the progress of the association and promote the happiness, well-being and usefulness of the membership, to exemplify and perpetuate those principles which have come to be regarded as the ideas and traditions of the industry." (*Telephone Pioneers of America Webpage*)

Each year, this group had a telephone insulator made in a different color and Imperial made these for several years. We have seen several different colors, but we have no list of the colors and years. Frank Moore, long-time mould maker for Imperial, made the mould for this production.

Telephone Insulators. These insulators were ordered annually for National Telephone Pioneers of America Human Services. The Milk Glass Insulators was made in 1971 for the 61st Anniversary of this group. Imperial made souvenirs in different colors each year for several years for the NTPA conventions. Frank Moore, long time mould maker for Imperial, made the mould for this production. $25-30.

West Virginia Centennial

West Virginia Centennial was one of the private mould customers that ordered the Glass Colonial Key paperweight. For them, the Key paperweight was made in Blue Satin. By placing different "word plugs" into the mould, the Key paperweight mould could be used for several customers.

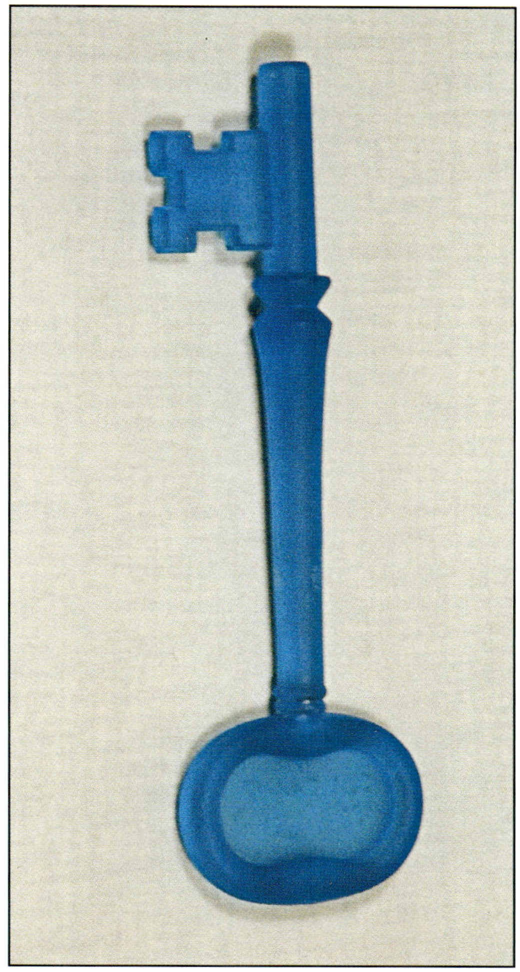

Glass Colonial Key Paperweight, Blue Satin.

Jamestown, Virginia

The Jamestown, Virginia, colony was established in 1607, and there the first glass was made in America in 1608. It was the first industry in the United States. Ed Gustkey, president of Imperial Glass Corporation, was instrumental in the restoration of the glasshouse at Jamestown.

Queen Elizabeth II of England went to Jamestown in May of 2007 to celebrate the 400th anniversary of the first English settlement in America.

Cathedral Arts Company: 1971

Cathedral Arts Company bought the Cape Cod cruet with a specially made cross stopper.

#160/119, Cape Cod cruet with a cross stopper, 1971-1976. $25-30.

Chaplains' Aid Association Inc.: 1952 to 1968

Chaplains' Aid Association Inc. bought the Cape Cod #160/29, 7" oblong Tray, 1952 to 1968. $20-30.

International Silver Company: 1968

International Silver Company ordered the #160/119 Cruet with Cross Stopper as well as the following items:

#1211, Punch Cup
#342, Epergne, Wired
#1489, Decanter Stopper
#1519/152, 5", Epergne
#1519/153, 6"

H. A. Framburg & Company: 1937

In 1937, H. A. Framburg & Company, of Chicago, Illinois, ordered glass lamp parts from Imperial. Framburg was established in 1905 and is still in business today. They make exquisite lighting fixtures and sell to the trade only.

We contacted Framburg in the 1990s and on invitation we visited this company. It was exciting to see the quality of light fixtures they make and to tour the workrooms.

Several items were sold to this company and included on a factory paper was this interesting description: "#5868 Crystal Ivory Shade, Ivory Enamel." We wonder if this #5868 could describe a Candlewick part, as we do know of Candlewick shades that resemble Imperial's products. We have been unable to document this one with the Ivory description. Does that pertain to Candlewick? (See page 136.)

Type A and B Bobesches
Type C Cylinder with Gray Cutting
#905 Crystal Urn
#791 Sand/blast and Cut
#G-112 Candlewick Saucer
#5868 Crystal, Ivory shade, Ivory enamel

II.
Glass Made From Imperial's Moulds For Customers To Alter Before Selling

Enchanting Lighting
Oneida, Ltd.
Superior Electric Products, Corp.
Keystone Silver, Inc.
H. L. Lamp Shade, Inc.
Nelson Bead Co.
Neiman Marcus
Guild Metal Company

Enchanting Lighting Company: 1938-1941

The Enchanting Lighting Company was a wholesale lighting company in New Orleans, Louisiana. They bought fixtures from Imperial Lighting Company [manufacturer] who was not a part of the Imperial Glass Company. In an Enchanting Lighting Company catalog #38 (possibly 1938), there is shown a ceiling fixture that uses a #699 Candy Jar, without the foot and with a hole in center of the bottom.

Laced Edge Shade,
Washington Dome (base of compote)
Empire Flat Plate

A factory paper indicated that the #699 Candy Jar without a foot, with a hole in bottom was sold to Imperial Lighting Product Company in 1941. (Refer to Lamp section on page 140. This same comport part was used as part of a ceiling fixture shown on page 141.)

Oneida, Ltd.: 1954-1967

A collector can build a sizeable collection by collecting Candlewick pieces boxed with a piece of Oneida Silverplate. Different patterns of Silverplate were used. Oneida bought from Imperial the following Candlewick items:

#400/49 Heart
#400/52B Bowl
#400/54 Relish
#400/257 Cheese Dish
#400/268 Relish

Superior Electric Products, Corporation: 1940s

Another of the many lighting companies that bought glass parts from Imperial Glass Corporation is Superior Electric Products, Corporation. In 1948 Superior Electric Products bought the #701 Reeded End Relish Dish. It is interesting to attempt to think how this two-part relish dish would be used in a lamp. Perhaps it is inset into a wood or metal part that is the base of the lamp. (See Chapter 2, Reeded section.)

Keystone Silver, Inc. New York, NY

The business name is Keystone Silver, Inc., New York, New York. However, the examples that we have either found or have received information about combined Candlewick and Wood rather than silver. The first example came from a couple I have not personally met, but that have shared several outstanding finds they found.

One find was the #400/65/2, Candlewick Candy Bottom with a wooden lid placed on a larger wooden tray with the Keystone Label on it.

Also found is a Punch Set with a raised ring in center to hold the bowl and another raised ring on either side of punch cup. Included in the set was the #400/74B 10" Bowl; #400/77AD After Dinner Cup; #400/139 Ladle on Wood Tray. A label on underside of tray has Keystone Silver, Inc.

H. L. Lamp Shade, Inc.

H.L. [Henry Lewis] Lamp Shade, Inc. The factory paper referring to this customer also had a hand written note by the area representative--"they purchase items and mount them on wood." Be on the lookout for an item combined with wood that fits one of the following Candlewick descriptions:

#400/1F, 5" Nappy
#400/58, 8" Pickle Tray
#400/276 Butter Base only

Nelson Bead Company: 1941

The Nelson Bead Company is a company name that we have searched for over the years. We have a factory paper dated 1941 naming items this company purchased from Imperial Glass. We have the table lamp made from these parts, but we have no other information on the company. Lamp shown on page 137.

#400/86 Mushroom Candleholder, bottom
#400/33 Individual Jelly, top
#451 Bud Vase, stem, from Imperial's general line (10" Bud Vase, no foot, and not cracked off)

Neiman Marcus, Dallas, Texas

Neiman Marcus is an upscale retailer in Dallas. A friend found three #400/419 Martini Pitchers and shared one of the finds with us. The Sterling Silver attached base is marked in script Neiman Marcus, Sterling and is followed by the number 70 engraved on it. The #400/419 Martini Pitcher is the No Bead Pitcher taken from the Continental Line.

Guild Metal

The mention of this company was the first and only company name that we have found to indicate Imperial Glass items were sold to a metal company to be combined with metal for sale to a secondary market. There was not any detailed information with the pattern numbers.

#695
#696
#697
#698 Monticello

Assortment of Colognes with Filigree, unknown distributors. $15-35.

Other Distributors

Glass pieces with filigree metal have been the most difficult to identify. Many of the dresser set items can be found with metal attached to them.

Cologne Bottles Sold to Perfumers or Metal Companies:

#282 Collectors Crystal Cologne Bottle with Puritan Cosmetics, St. Louis, Missouri label.

#699 Washington Cologne Bottle with label on bottom "Tinsley's of Nashville," and "SS Pierce Company." Pierce Co. was found on a Private Mould list in 1940. Pierce is an importer of gourmet teas and foods.

#160/177 Cape Cod Condiment bottle has a label "Fabulous Boutique Originals by Robert."

Unknown Distributors

#975, Candy Dish with metal lid. This is the same candy dish bottom in found in the Ruby Flashed ceiling fixture and the Marigold Shade. $15-20.

R-920, 10" Footed Bottle and Stopper. It is one piece of a three-piece set. It was made in Crystal, Rose, and Blue. The metal company that placed the metal is unknown. In the photograph, the metal reflected in the crystal making it a yellow tint

III.

Glass Blanks Sold to Companies to Decorate and Sell As Their Own Products

Glastonbury Decorating, Company
Lotus Decorating Company
Wheeling Decorating Company
Able, Wasserberg & Company
W. J. Hughes Company
Silver City Glass Company
Flemington Cut Glass Company
Royal Lancer
National Silver Deposit Company

Glastonbury Company, Chicago, Illinois: 1930-1940s

Glastonbury Company, Chicago, Illinois, bought blanks from glass companies and decorated them to sell as their own product. It seems that most of the business between Glastonbury and Imperial was during the years 1939 and 1943. The decoration that we can document is one with three narrow 22K gold lines and a wider outer line of gold.

Lotus Decorating Company, Barnesville, Ohio, bought Glastonbury in 1960. Lotus also bought blanks that included Candlewick from Imperial Glass Company. Lotus did the following decorations on those blanks:

Bridal Bouquet #906 Etch
Buttercup #116GB Etch
Oak Leaf #72 Silver Deposit

Wheeling Decorating Company, Wheeling, West Virginia

Another company that bought blanks from Imperial was Wheeling Decorating Company. Some of the glass may have been sold as a product for Wheeling Decorating. Others were decorated by Wheeling Decorating to be sold as an Imperial product. Companies often exchanged glass making and decorating.

One of the decorations was an etched design, "Woodland" Etch [Dog Scene] on a #400/31 Sugar and Creamer.

Another decoration was a hand-painted series of a Horse with Rider Jumping Hurdles on Imperial's #142 Tumbler.

Abels, Wasserberg and Company: 1940s

Abels, Wasserberg and Company, sold hand-painted roses on glass in the 1940s under the descriptive name "Charleton." Charleton painting can be found on the following Imperial Candlewick items:

#400/103C, 10" Footed Fruit Bowl
#400/110, Candy Box & Cover
#400/140 ,Candy Box & Cover
#400/75, Salad Fork & Spoon
#400/149F, 7 ½" Handled Bon Bon
#400/150, 6" Ash Tray

W.J. Hughes, Canada

One of the best-known decorators to buy from Imperial was a glasscutter in Canada, W.J. Hughes, Ltd. This company cut their famous Corn Flower design on glass blanks bought from various companies. Imperial sold a considerable amount of blanks to Hughes. Candlewick was by far the largest order for blanks to a decorator for which we have records. This story is covered fully in *Elegant Glass with Corn Flower,* Schiffer Publishing, Ltd. by Walter Lemiski.

Silver City Glass Company

Silver City Glass Company applied 22k and 24k Silver and Gold Overlay designs to pieces of glass. Collectors today are still finding these items with the labels intact. Two examples are following:

#75 Candleholder with Silver Overlay Pattern of Grapes and Leaves. Label states Sterling on Glass Non Tarnish.

#142 Tumbler with label stating 22k Gold Decoration.

Flemington Cut Glass Company, Flemington, New Jersey.

Established in the early 1900s was the Flemington Cut Glass Company, Flemington, New Jersey. We purchased #400/72B, 8 1/2" Bowl with a Flemington label on it. At the time of purchase, the factory outlet told us "Carroll" was the name of the cut.

Royal Lancer Sterling Silver

We have an example of this in *Candlewick: Colored and Decorated*. It is the #400/247 with the wide silver band around the top area of the salt and pepper. The insert in the box gave instructions, "When the silver needs polishing use Glass Wax or mix precipitated chalk with water until it becomes a paste. Rub on with a soft cloth. Allow to dry and wipe with a clean soft cloth."

National Silver Deposit Ware Company, Inc.: 1940s

National Silver Deposit Ware Company, Inc. 1941. #142, #630 Decanter with Cuts, #8711, #8701 and #1748

IV.

Glass Made From Imperial's Moulds in Non-production Colors

T. Eaton Company, Ltd.
DeVilbiss Company
Ocean Spray Cranberry Company
Star Exclusive, Inc.
Levay Distributors
Lipman Sterling, Ltd.
Earl W. Newton
Baumgartner Apple Orchard
Koscherak Bros.
Mirror Images, O. J. Scherschligt
Weil Ceramic
G.A. Westphal Co.

T. Eaton Company, Ltd., Ontario, Canada: 1950s

T. Eaton Company, Ltd. purchased the Reeded #701 Salad Fork and Spoon in Black in 1954. They also bought the #400/96 Salt in Green and Violet and the #400/167 Salt in Violet.

DeVilbiss Company, Toledo, Ohio: 1938

DeVilbiss made and sold bottles and all types of spray attachments for medical equipment. The company was started in 1898 by Dr. Allen DeVilbiss when he invented an easier way to apply medicine to patient's throats. From medical sprays of all types, they progressed to paint sprays, air sprayers, and other large sprayers. The sons were doctors and inventors. We found a great history of DeVilbiss on the internet for this information. It did not include mention of perfume bottles, but we know that they also had this line because they bought Candlewick #400/96, #400/167 and #400/267 Salt and Peppers in several colors. On the bottom of some of the bottles are the DeVilbiss labels; 1952-1953.

Ocean Spray Cranberry Company, Lakeville-Middleboro, Massachusetts: 1969

In 1969, Ocean Spray Cranberry, bought the Cape Cod 160/105 Oval Relish in the color Azalea. In the past, they have purchased various items for sale in the gift shop. Ocean Spray Cranberry might have purchased the Azalea Relish for the gift shop.

Star Exclusive, Inc. New Orleans, Louisiana: 1976 - 1977

Imperial Glass Corporation had a contract to make over fifty items exclusively for Star Exclusives, Inc., a proposed party-plan company in New Orleans. The IG hallmark was to be removed from all of the items made.

Twenty-five items were to be included in sample kits for the salespeople. The original order was to be four kits of each of the twenty-five items, followed by ninety-six additional sample kits. We understood that Star Exclusives, Inc. went bankrupt before receiving the sample kits. It is unknown how many items were produced, but it seems that it could have been a limited number.

The following list shows items in the catalog printed for the sales promotion. The names and numbers given are just as they appeared in the sales promotion. The pattern identification numbers are as they shown in the catalog. Prism was the name given to the #699 Washington Line. The authors supplied information in the brackets.

Amberglo Collection

#55891AM, Footed Jar and Cover
#55722AM, Turn O' The Century Compote
#55900AM, Hootie Decorator "Owl" and Cover
#55700AM, Cape Cod 12" Bowl, [#160/75B without hand shaped flare]
#55420AM, Cape Cod 14" Platter [#160/75D]
#55682AM, 3-Toed Rose Bowl 7 1/2"
#55906AM, Honey Pot with Cover 5 1/2"
#55646AM, Cape Cod Basket 11", [#160/40]

Ultra Blue Collection

#55856UB, Spirit of America, Eagle Ash Tray
#55712UB, Spirit of America, Eagle Cigarette Holder
#55690UB, Center Piece Bowl, 8 3/4"
#55320UB, Spirit of America, Eagle Mug
#55750UB, Hobnail Glo Lamp
#55840UB, Hobnail Bell
#55760UB, Flowered Decorator Celery
#55903UB, Springerle Covered Sweets Bowl

Crystal Collection

#55570CRY, 3 Partitioned Jeweled Covered Server
#55528CRY, 3" Cornucopia
#55644CRY, Daisy Basket, 9 1/2"
#55720CRY, Daisy Footed Comport

Amberina Collection

#55894RU, Candy Jar, 6 1/2"
#55882RU, 9" Cookie Jar
#55680RU, Berry Nucut Bowl, 8"
#55764RU, 2-handled Celery Vase 6 1/2"
#55638RU, Decorator Urn 8 1/2"
#55990RU, 2-piece Handled Candle Lamp
#55640RU, Flowered Basket
#55382RU, Windmill Wall or Luncheon Plate 9"

Verde Green Collection

#55170VE, Cape Cod Wine Decanter and Stopper, [#160/163, 30 oz.]
#55241VE, Cape Cod Wine Glass, [1602, 5 oz. Wine]
#55420VE, Cape Cod Platter 14", [#160/75D]
#55458VE, Cape Cod Basket, [#160/221/0, 9"]
#55410VE, Prism Cake Plate 12", [#699]
#55475VE, Lady and Gentleman Salz and Pieffer
#55692VE, Prism Salad Bowl 10", [#699]
#55531VE, Prism Covered Sugar, [#699]
#55534VE, Prism Cream Pitcher, [#699]
#55885VE, Candy Box and Cover
#55783VE, Cape Cod Candleholders, [#160/170]
#55585VE, Cape Cod Relish and Dressing Set, #160/1112, [insert bowl is Crystal]
#55610VE, Prism Butter and Cover, [#699]
#55470VE, Prism Salt and Pepper, [#699]
#55090VE, Prism 12 oz. Glass, [#699]
#55150VE, Prism 54 oz. Pitcher, [#699]

Nut Brown Collection

#55850NB, Decorator Trivet Set
#55762NB, 8" Vase Nucut
#55710NB, Cigarette Lighter, [#1602 Cape Cod Cordial]
#55754VB, Diamond Cut Vase
#55888NB, Jeweled Covered Box
#55642NB, Miniature Basket 5 1/2"
#55752NB, Loganberry Vase 8"
#55820NB, Toothpick Holder
#55897NB, Dewey Box and Cover

Levay Distributing Company: 1970s

Imperial made several Cape Cod items for Levay, a glass mail-order company.

The #160/70 Cruets, Pointed Stopper, Marigold, Needle etched on bottom, "Levay, 1 of 300, [and this one was marked #177.] 1977." It can also is also found with the fancy round stopper.

There have been Punch Cups and Tumblers found in Marigold, but we are unsure if they, too, were made for Levay.

The Lipman Sterling, Ltd. Toronto, Canada: 1940s-1950s

Lipman Sterling, Ltd. bought decorated Candlewick #3400 stems from Imperial in 1949. They may have bought other blanks, also, but these Candlewick stems are the only ones that we have a record.

#400 Candlewick
#160 Cape Cod
#800
#788

Imperial decorated the #3400 stems with the same design for Imperial's line as well as for Lipman. If the item were for Imperial's line, the etched design would have a gold line edge added to it. The design would have a different name when it was without the gold edge made for Lipman. The names for these designs follow:

Grape #6 is an etched without gold edge for Lipman
With gold edge, it was Catawba for Imperial line.
Thistle #10 is etched without gold for Lipman
With gold edge, it was Dalmally Thistle for Imperial line.
Fernwood #2 is etched without gold edge for Lipman
With gold edge, it was Minton Band for Imperial line.

Various Salt and Pepper set without tops were ordered by Lipman. This would account for many Imperial glass salt and pepper sets that appear with sterling lids rather than the usual chrome or plastic lids put on by Imperial Glass.

Earl W. Newton, Bowling Green, Ohio: 1960s

Former Imperial President, Earl W. Newton, maintained a glass and china show room in Chicago, Illinois. He was Imperial's president from 1931 to early 1940s During the time he was president he continued his Chicago Showroom. In the 1940s, he started promoting hand-painted glass to match some of the china and pottery lines represented by his showroom.

Are you familiar with Blue Ridge Pottery of the 1930s-1950s? Collectors can find inexpensive glass sherbets and glasses with hand-painting that resembles some hand painting done by Imperial. As early collectors of Blue Ridge as well as Candlewick, we strongly believe that Imperial did the painting on glass to go with some of the Blue Ridge patterns made by Southern Potteries.

When we found a factory paper indicating that Mr. Newton was a customer of Imperial's in 1960, we felt that there was a connection. Did he have Federal Glass blanks decorated at Imperial or did he send his decorators to Imperial to learn the techniques? The mention in the records gave an address of Bowling Green, Ohio, which was his hometown. Maybe this sparse mention will lead someone else to find the rest of this story.

After Earl W. Newton stepped down as president of Imperial Glass Company, he returned to his Chicago office where he represented Imperial Glass Company, Southern Potteries, and other brands of glass, potteries, and china and gift items. Because of this multiple connection, it is probable that this was the source of the marriage of hand-painted glass items to match some of the Blue Ridge Pottery. Painting on the glass items that complement Blue Ridge strongly resemble the quality of the hand-painting on Imperial Glass.

Baumgartner Apple Orchard

A good friend, a former bookkeeper of Imperial, shared the find of the #400/28C, Candlewick vase. It has the hand-painted Western Apple design on it. We assume that these items were made for this customer to use as gifts. That we know of, there are three items painted for this company. Along with the vase, we acquired a piece of Baumgartner Apple Orchard stationary. It has a big red apple printed in the corner. Items found have been:

#400/63B, 10 ½" Bowl
#400/106B, 12" Bowl
#400/28C, 8 ½" footed Bud Vase

Koscherak Brothers: 1940s

On one factory paper, there is a description of hand-painted items sold to Koscherak Brothers, in the 1940s. This paper allowed us to know that our items and items found by others were Imperial decorations.

Peach Blossom with Gold and Blue Violets without Gold were painted on these items:

#400/79 Hurricane
#592 Cologne & Puff Candy Box

Mirror Images, O.J. Scherschligt, Lansing, Michigan

Ten Animals were a special order from Imperial for Mirror Images, which is owned by O.J. Scherschligt. These animals were ordered in Cobalt, but that did not happen. Due to problems with the glass color, Imperial only made in Cobalt the following animals: Airedale, Gazelle, Donkey, Medium Elephant, Scottie, and Woodchuck.

Because Imperial was having difficulty with the Cobalt glass, the Mother Pig and Piglets were taken to Wetzel Glass for production in Cobalt. To finish the group of ten animals Imperial made the Filly Head Forward and the Clydesdale in Amber.

Before Mr. Scherschligt took ownership of the Clydesdale, Imperial entered into bankruptcy. During liquidation, Consolidated Colony contacted Mr. Scherschligt and reached an agreement for the sale of the Clydesdale.

Besides the Animals, Imperial made the Venus Rising in twelve colors in glossy and satin. The original Cambridge Bashful Charlotte Flower Frog mould was used. Imperial made these without holes and added ribs around base to differentiate the Imperial product and the Cambridge product.

After Imperial Glass Corporation, Mr. Scherschligt turned to Dalzell Viking Glass Company and then to Mosser Glass, Inc. for the production of his animals.

Weil Ceramic

Imperial decorated a #158 Canapé Plate Decorated with Daisy and Gold Eagle design. We do not know if a collector has found this example. Weil Ceramic placed an order for this item.

G.A. Westphal Company

G.A. Westphal Company purchased the following items to be decorated with Cornfield:

#110 Stems, Twist
#8701 Tumblers, has to be a plain tumbler
#176 Pitchers, Continental
#85 & #2428 Plates, plain used for cutting
#3400 Seafood Icer, Candlewick

V.

Glass Made From Imperial Moulds For A Customer to Market As Its Own Product

Quaker Oats, Company, Chicago, Illinois
Paramount Trading Co.
Butler Brothers, Chicago, Illinois
Old Sturbridge Village, Sturbridge, Massachusetts
Oriental Trading Company, Omaha, Nebraska
Newland Schneelock and Piek
Sears Roebuck Company
F.W. Woolworth Company

Quaker Oats, Company, Chicago, Illinois: 1931

There is Quaker Oats box that would be over 75 Years Old! It once contained the Imperial Cape Cod premium items. Originally, seven pieces of Cape Cod were given as premiums in Mother's Oats. Eventually, Imperial designed and made over 300 pieces of the impressive crystal. The story of Cape Cod is fully covered in *Imperial Cape Cod*.

Paramount Premium Company: 1937

The Paramount Premium Company purchased nine Mt. Vernon, #699, items and 2 Laced Edge items in 1937. Mt. Vernon was renamed Washington. Paramount Premium Company may have purchased more than the following list:

#6992, Goblet
#6992, Sherbet
#699, 12 oz. Ice Tea Tumbler
#6990D, 8" Round Plate
#6993W, 4 3/4" Fruit
#6990, Sugar
#6990, Cream
#6997B, 8 1/2" Bowl
#6997D, 11" Plate
#7498D, 12" Plate (Laced Edge)
#749, Twin-candlestick (Laced Edge)

Butler Brothers, Chicago, Illinois: 1937-1940s

Another of the largest customers of Imperial was Butler Brothers. In 1937, records indicate that Butler Brothers bought pieces from the following lines. A complete list of each pattern is too extensive to be covered in full detail. We believe that it is adequate for collectors to know that Butler Brothers bought these patterns in various colors.

#330, "Diamond Block," Venetian Blue
#330, "Diamond Block," Crystal
#745 Laced Edge, Ruby
#555, Nucut, Crystal

As early as 1937, Butler Brothers, a mail order catalog company, ordered twelve pieces of the #701, Reeded pattern in Crystal, Amber, and Hock Green. Following is a list of that group:

#701/1, Squat Rose Bowl, 5"
#701/2, Rose Bowl, 6"
#701/4, Tall Vase, 9"
#701, 2-pc. Sugar and Cream
#701, 3-pc. Mayo Set
#70181B, Bowl, snap bottom, 10"
#70181D, Plate, snap bottom 12"
#701, Candlestick
#701, Candy Box with Cover
#7018B, 10" Deep Belled Bowl, ground bottom, Crystal, Hock Green, and Amber.
#7018D, 14" Plate, ground bottom, Crystal, Hock Green, and Amber.

Already collectors know that six items of the popular Candlewick #400 line were made for Butler Brothers. These pieces were produced in Black with Cosmos decoration exclusively for Butler Brothers. In addition, the six items were made in Ruby and in Crystal with a cut design. The list of Candlewick is as follows:

400/62D, 8 1/4" 2-handle Plate
400/62E, 8 1/4" 2-handle Tray
400/62EC, 8 1/4" 2-handle Dish
400/74B, 8 1/4" 4-Toed Nappy
400/74SC, 8" 4-Toed Fancy Dish
400/74N, 7" Flower Bowl

Butler Brothers ordered other patterns from Imperial. Line numbers, dates, and colors will be listed when it is known.

#275, 8 1/2" Oval Tray, Ruby
#5285/111
#710, Viennese Blue, Block
#134, Bubbles, Ruby

Pillar Flute

#10/682 Sugar, Ruby
#10/682, Cream, Ruby
#10/682, 6" 2-handle Pickle, Ruby
#10/6825A, 6" round Bowl, Ruby
#10/6825C, 7" crimped Nappy, Ruby
#10/682, 4 1/2", 2-handled Nappy, Ruby

#698, Monticello

#698, Goblet, Crystal

#698, Sherbet. Crystal
#698, 12 oz. Tumbler, Crystal
#698D, 8" Salad Plate, Crystal
#698, 5 1/2" Cream Soup, 2-handled, Crystal
#698, 4 1/2" Finger Bowl, Crystal
#698, 5 1/2" Bon Bon, single handle, Crystal
#698, 6" Oval Pickle and under plate, Crystal
#698, Open Sugar and Cream, Crystal
#698B, Stem Cocktail, Crystal
#698F, 5 1/2" Comport, Crystal
#6981W, 5 1/2" Ice or Butter Tub, (slightly tapered out) Crystal
#698N, 6" Lily Bowl, Crystal
#698, Tall Candy Jar and Cover, Crystal, also Ruby Cover
#698, Large Butter and Cover, Crystal
#698, 5 1/2" Comport, Crystal, Crystal
#6982 Tall Candy Jar and Cover, Crystal
#6980D, 8" Plate, round, Ruby
#6983D, 6" Plate, round, Ruby
#6987D, 10 1/2" Plate, round, Ruby

#699, Mt. Vernon, 10 pc. Set [no information]

Color names mentioned during 1937-1940 productions were Ruby, Venetian Blue, Meadow Green, and Rose Pink, but we do not have other specifics for all of those names. We hope that knowing the pattern design and possible Imperial colors will assist collectors.

Mt Vernon, #699 AKA Washington, when sold to Butler Brothers in 1938, #699 was named Early American. This only adds to the confusion of Imperial identification of this pattern name. The Early American items were:
#6990F, 7" Shallow Nappy
#6990N, 5" Flower Bowl
#699, 5 3/4" One-handled Bon Bon
#6991, 5 3/4", 2-handled Nappy
#6995W, 7" Square Nappy
#699, 6" Two-handled Pickle
#6991W, 5" Open Tub
#6990, Open Sugar
#6990, Cream
#699F, 6" Comport

#710 Block AKA Beaded Block
#710, Block, Viennese Blue
#710, 4 3/4" Two-handled Nappy
#710, 6 1/2" Two handled Pickle
#710, 5 1/2" One-handled Olive
#7105B, 6 1/2" Belled Nappy
#710, 8 1/2" Oval Celery Tray
#7105N, 5" Flower Bowl
#710, 5 1/2" Square Dish
#710, 8" Square Plate

#749, Twin-Candlestick to go with set

Empire, #779
#779 Candy Box and Cover, Ruby
#7796SC, 9" Square Bowl, Venetian Blue
#7796D, 10" Plate, Venetian Blue
#7796M, 6" Lily Bowl
#7796W, 8" Flared Bowl

"Molly" #725, AKA "Molly": 1930s and 1940
#4/7255W, 6", 2-handled Nappy, Black with Daisy decoration
#4/7255D, 7 1/4", 2-handled Plate, Black with Daisy decoration
#7257W9/118, 2-pc., Salad Set
#72510D/118, 2-handled Plate, 15"

#666, AKA "Huckabee" AKA "Cane," Crystal: 1940
#666B, 8 1/2" Belled Nappy
#666S, 8 1'2" Square Nappy
#666, 8 1/2" Celery Tray
#6665, 5 1/2" 2-handled Jelly
#666, 2-handled Oval Comport
#666, 6" Footed Bouquet

This list is of interest to Candleholder collectors. In 1940, Butler Brothers bought these Candlesticks:
#153, Twin Candlestick
#749, Laced Edge Twin Candlestick
#780, Laced Edge, Twin Candlestick
#779, Empire, Single Dolphin, Empire
#41, Single Candlestick
#677, 7" Single Candlestick

Old Sturbridge Village, Sturbridge, Massachusetts

The Old Sturbridge Village bought several Imperial items for sale in their mail-order catalog in 1982:

#61405, Give Us This Day Our Daily Bread, Plate
#61206, Ribbed Palm Goblet
#160, Tradition Birthday Cake Plate (footed)
#160, Cape Cod Stems
#341, Old Williamsburg Stems

#61405, Give Us This Day Our Daily Bread, Plate. $30-40.

Oriental Trading Company, Omaha, Nebraska

Oriental Trading Company started business in 1932 and is still in business today. According to the company website, "Oriental Trading is the nation's leading direct marketer of value-priced novelties, toys, and party supplies, and a leading direct marketer of home décor products." It is interesting to note the information that this company sells home décor products. We know that Imperial sold this company some products in 1938.

There are three product groups sold to this company that leave some questions unanswered. The Imperial factory page for Oriental Trading Company did not indicate what the Intaglio Gift Assortment included nor did it tell what the Novelty Gift Set comprised.

We do know that there was the #134 Olive Gift Assortment, but we do not know what pieces it contained. It is interesting that the same page itemized the Reeded #701 items.

Olive #134 was made in Hock Green, Amber, Ritz Blue, Ruby, and Crystal.

#701, 3-pc. Mayo
#701, 5 pc. Cigarette Set
#701, Covered Candy
#701, Candlestick, 3"
#701, Rose Vase, 5"
#701, Bubble Ball Vase, 6"
Intaglio Gift Assortment 4 pc.
Novelty Gift Set 3-pc.
#134, Olive Gift Assortment

Newland, Schneelock & Piek

Company records indicated that the Cut #279 "will be sold only by Newland, Schneelock & Piek." Perhaps it meant that these items with the #279 Cut were only sold to this company. On the other hand, it could be that these were the early items with this cut and sold exclusively to Newland, Schneelock & Piek. Imperial did use this cut on Candlewick in its general line.

#400/31, Sugar and Cream
#400/40, 3-pc. Mayo
#400/49, Candy & Cover
#400/54, 6 1/2" Relish
#400/55, 8 1/2" Relish
#400/56, 10 1/2" Relish
#400/66B" Comport
#400/72B, 8 1/2" 2-handle Bowl
#400/72D, 10" 2-handle Plate
#400/82, Cheese & Cracker
#400/87F, 8" Vase
#400/89, 4-pc. Marmalade

More items sold to Newland, Schneelock & Piek in 1938 include these Pillar Flute items:

#682, 5" Cigarette Box & 3 1/2" Square Ash Tray
#682, 5" Cigarette Box & 5" Oblong Ash Tray
#682, Puff Box
#682, Cologne

Sears Roebuck & Company: 1940s

Sears Roebuck & Company bought Laced Edge in 1943 and promoted it as the name, Crocheted. An Imperial advertising flyer stated, "Our own name for the elegantly famous old design now reproduced exclusively for Sears Roebuck in new beauty, brilliance, and variety." The Laced Edge pattern is fully covered in *Imperial Lace Edge,* Schiffer Publishing, Ltd. author Laura Marsh.

The identifying characteristic of Laced Edge is the open loops around the outer edge. Laced Edge items have several different designs added and those distinguishing featured are following:

#743 Diamond Points with and without Intaglio
#745 Diamond Points and small Buttons mixed
#749 Small triangles
#780 Panel Optic with and without Intaglio bottoms

Sears Roebuck also purchased line #165, Tradition from Imperial in the 1939 and 1940. Sears sold the Tradition pattern under the name Georgian. It is interesting that Sears sold the #165 Pitcher along with the Cape Cod line. They do not show it with the "Georgian" Line.

Sears list is as follows:

#165, Goblet 7 1/2 oz.
#165, Sherbet 4 1/2 oz.
#165, Wine 2 oz.
#165, Iced Tea, 12 oz.
#1655D, Salad Plate 8"
#1654 1/2D, Salad Plate 7"
#165B, Cocktail
#1654 1/2X, Baked Apple 6"
#1654 1/2A, Finger Bowl 4 1/2"

F.W. Woolworth Company

F.W. Woolworth Company was a volume buyer of Imperial Glass. Their business relations covered the period 1905-1935. Again, detailed information was not on the papers we had for reference. It is important to have even sparse information that gives us a general idea.

Remember that pattern names shown in quotation marks are not Imperial names, but are names given by early Depression glass researcher Hazel Marie Weatherman. The names she used gave collector a means of communication that is often easier to remember that numbers.

#212 Nucut, 12 items
#555 Nucut, 12 items
#503 Bellaire, First introduced exclusively for F.W. Woolworth.
#612 First introduced exclusively for F.W. Woolworth
#671 Number only mentioned
#330 "Diamond Block" [added by sales representative] "best line without doubt, 12 items."
#313 "Twisted Optic"
#719 "Lindberg" F.W. Woolworth. 75 Anniversary, 16 items
#721 "Scroll Fluted," 19 items
#95 6 items

VI.

Glass Made For Customers' Business Use

Restaurant and Hotel Trade: 1960s

Another interesting avenue of merchandising for Imperial was its restaurant trade. We have only one packet of information on this and it covers 1962-1964. It is a compilation of items from Imperial's general line that Imperial sent out to the Restaurant and Hotel trade with the notation that:

> These items are currently most popular with such customers. We have many other items from Salt Dips to Punch Bowls. Please tell us your needs. We will be glad to make items "especially" for you. We can cut, screen, hand-decorate, sandblast, acid-frost or etch. If you need, a special "crest" on a Goblet, Tumblers, etc. please send a drawing of the crest and we will be glad to quote prices. We make 15 different colors.

Over two hundred items were offered in the following categories; pitchers, tumblers, goblets, liners, covers, plates, salt and pepper sets, cruets, relishes, coasters, and ash trays

Tiki Stem TIKE, Private Mould Customer.

One of the items that we purchased during the liquidation of Imperial's assets in 1984 was the #530X, 2 oz. Sherry Stem for the Hotel Muehlebach, Kansas City, Missouri. This blank is shown in the Hotel and Barware, Catalogue No. 101 Blown and Pressed, Hand Made Glassware, Manufactured by Imperial Glass Corporation, Central Division, Bellaire, Ohio.

Trader Vic Restaurants

Trader Vic's is one of the notable restaurants that bought in the 1960s. Some of the items offered were from Imperial's General Line. Items offered exclusively for Trader Vic's were:

#2057 Cocktail, Plain, Amber Stem
#2057 Cocktail, Optic, Amber Stem
#2057 Large Sherbet, Amber Stem
#2060 Cocktail, Black Stem

Hotel Muhlebach, Kansas City, Missouri

One of the items that we purchased during the liquidation of Imperial's assets in 1984 was the #530X, 2 oz. Sherry stem for the Hotel Muehlebach, Kansas City, Missouri. This blank is shown in the Hotel and Barware, Catalog No. 101 Blown and Pressed, Hand Made Glassware, Manufactured by Imperial Glass Corporation, Central Division, Bellaire, Ohio. The stem has the Muehlebach emblem and information acid etched on the Sherry.

Private Organizations

Various Private Organizations bought items from Imperial. Individuals, Fraternal Organizations, and Civic Groups were among those groups. Often the name or symbols of the group decorated the items.

Advertising Ash Trays seemed to be a popular way to advertise, particularly in the 1950-1960s. One such Ash Tray pictured the Union Savings Bank, Bellaire, Ohio. Now this building is the Imperial Glass Museum

A few examples of personalized Ash Trays are:

#400/118, Between Place Ash Tray, Walter C. Baukneght, Bellaire Ohio, 1966
#400/150, Ash Tray, First National Bank, Bellaire, Ohio
#400/150, Ash Tray, Greek Letters, Alpha Pi Sigma
#400/133, Ash Tray, Pilot International
#400/133, Ladies Silhouette

Just a few of the many souvenirs:

#400/172, 4 ½" Heart Mould
#400/172, 1974 Blue
#400/172, 1975 Green
#400/172, 1976 Milk Glass
#400/172, 1977 Amber

Sold in Cuba

While not considered a private mould customer, Imperial had a factory representative in Cuba until 1962. Some of the lines sold in Cuba include:

#160, Cape Cod
#212, Nucut
#737
#505
#388

Continental Silver

#779, 3" Bowl

Waterman and Leder Corp.

#400/20, punch cup

Bechtel, Lutz & Jost, Inc.

#400, Candlewick
#474
#612
#505
#671

Customers

In the last of this section are a few names that we found in a list of customers. There were no files or papers with this group. We think it is important to know that there was at least a business connection with these companies. This might help in future research.

Pavel and Co., New York. was a name that we know. There is a possibility that it is responsible for the Cranberry Flashed cut to clear 400/119 Cruet. This has been discussed often among Candlewick collectors. The cruets are shown in a Pavel advertisement with a line explaining, "Czech artisans decorated them in an American factory." Indeed many of these artisans immigrated to the United States and worked in the many glass factories. However, the cruets are the Imperial Glass Candlewick cruet and some of the Czechoslovakian artisans worked at Imperial.

The rest of the customer list we have included the following:

R.H. Macy
Marion Glass Company
Morgantown Glass Guild
S. Ortner
Schiller and Sons, Inc
Sharpe, Inc.
Sterling Glass
Paul A. Straub and Co.
R. Wallace and Sons Mfg.
Weiss and Beheller

Boyd Art Glass Company

The authors were a private mould customer to Boyd's Art Glass Company in Cambridge, Ohio. We wanted a nut cup to use at our 50th wedding anniversary dinner held at Wilson Lodge, Oglebay Park, Wheeling, West Virginia in 1998. Indiana Glass Company kept the Cape Cod moulds when they liquated Imperial Glass Company in 1985. They loaned us the #160/156, Bottom to the Mustard, Cape Cod mould in order for Boyd Art Glass to reproduce it in blue slag. This was limited to a run of approximately 200 pieces. We had attended our first National Imperial Glass Collectors' Society Convention at the lodge in 1982. The cups are marked for Bob & Myrna Garrison, with "B & M 50th."

Memorabilia

One must find a conclusion to end a story, and we will do that by showing a little Imperial memorabilia. Enjoy! We do not claim to have complete information on any subject we have researched since our beginning in 1980.

We hope that at least some little piece of information in this book will help you to identify your item and help you know if it was made by Imperial and/or it is part of an after-factory item.

Shown is a small group of Imperial's various advertising items. There are Decks of cards, Matches, Billfold, a Desk Diary, Thermometer, and Pencils.

Imperial Sign from the 1960s. Painted on textured glass. $*.

Certificate

No. C 999

For ______ Shares

Issued to

Dated ______ 19__

FROM WHOM TRANSFERRED

Dated ______ 19__

NO. ORIGINAL CERTIFICATE	NO. ORIGINAL SHARES	NO. OF SHARES TRANSFERRED

Received Certificate No. ______

For ______ Shares

this ______ day of ______ 19__

INCORPORATED UNDER THE GENERAL CORPORATION ACT OF THE STATE OF OHIO

No. C 999

Imperial Glass Corporation

Consolidated with Domestic Investment Company, January 7, 1939

AUTHORIZED SHARES:

FIRST PREFERRED, 1500 SHARES, PAR VALUE $100.00 EACH
SECOND PREFERRED, 4000 SHARES, PAR VALUE $25.00 EACH
COMMON, 1800 SHARES, PAR VALUE $25.00 EACH
Total par value of First Preferred Shares, $150,000.00
Total par value of Second Preferred Shares, $100,000.00
Total par value of Common Shares, $45,000.00

THIS IS TO CERTIFY that ......

is the owner of ...... COMMON SHARES of the par value of $25.00 each, fully paid and non-assessable, of Imperial Glass Corporation, transferable only on the books of the corporation, in person, or by duly authorized Attorney, upon surrender of this certificate properly endorsed.

A full statement of the terms, provisions, conditions, designations, preferences, restrictions and voting powers respectively of the First Preferred Shares, Second Preferred Shares and Common Shares, as contained in the Consolidation Agreement dated January 7, 1939, is set forth upon the reverse side of this certificate; and the shares hereby evidenced are issued and shall be held subject to all of said provisions, to which, by acceptance of this certificate, the holder hereof assents and agrees.

IN WITNESS WHEREOF, said IMPERIAL GLASS CORPORATION has caused this certificate to be signed by its duly authorized officers and its corporate seal to be hereunto affixed at Bellaire, Ohio, this ...... day of ......, 19......

SECRETARY   PRESIDENT

Common

Stock Certificate. Do you fell that you own stock in Imperial Glass Company because you have collected so much Imperial glass. Maybe this certificate will make you feel better.

Bibliography

Archer, Margaret and Douglas. *Imperial Glass Company*. Paducah, Kentucky: Collector Books, 1978.

Burns, Carl O. *Imperial Carnival Glass*. Paducah, Kentucky: Collector Books, 1996.

Marsh, Laura J. *Imperial Glass: Lace Edge*. Atglen, Pennsylvania: Schiffer Publishing, Ltd., 2004.

Garrison, Myrna and Bob. *Candlewick: Colored and Decorated*. Atglen, Pennsylvania: Schiffer Publishing, Ltd., 2003.

_____. *Candlewick: The Crystal Line*. Atglen, Pennsylvania: Schiffer Publishing, Ltd. 2005.

_____. *Imperial Cape Cod*. Atglen, Pennsylvania: Schiffer Publishing, Ltd., 2004.

_____. *Imperial's Boudoir, Etcetera. A Comprehensive Look at Dresser Accessories for Irice and Others*. Privately published, 1996.

_____. *Milk Glass, Imperial Glass Corporation*. Atglen, Pennsylvania: Schiffer Publishing, Ltd, 2001.

Imperial Glass Company, Imperial Glass Corporation, Cards File Copies, Catalogs, Notes, Price Guides, and Photographs. 1904-1982.

Lemiski, Walter. *Elegant Glass With Corn Flower.* Atglen, Pennsylvania: Schiffer Publishing, Ltd. 2005.

Measell, James, ed. *Imperial Glass Encyclopedia, Vol. I*. National Imperial Glass Collectors' Society. Marietta, Ohio: The Glass Press Inc., 1995.

_____. *Imperial Glass Encyclopedia, Vol. II*. National Imperial Glass Collectors' Society. Marietta, Ohio: The Glass Press Inc. 1997.

_____. *Imperial Glass Encyclopedia, Vol. III*. National Imperial Glass Collectors' Society. Marietta, Ohio: The Glass Press Inc. 1999.

Taves, Nathan & Jennings, Don. *Slag & Marble Glass, The Prominent Years, 1959-1985*. Atglen, Pennsylvania: Schiffer Publishing, Ltd., 2007.

Weatherman, Hazel Marie. *Colored Glassware of the Depression Era 2*. Springfield, Missouri: Weatherman Glassbooks, 1974.

Notes

More Schiffer Titles

www.schifferbooks.com

Imperial Cape Cod Glass. Myrna and Bob Garrison. The Cape Cod pattern by Imperial Glass Corporation began life as a Mother's Oats premium in 1932 and was manufactured until Imperial closed in 1984. Documented here are place settings, serving pieces, accessories, items made for private mold customers, and more. Detailed captions provide mold numbers, descriptions, significant information, and current values. A separate price guide lists all the crystal items. An invaluable reference for Imperial collectors and all who enjoy fine glassware.

Size: 8 1/2" x 11" 423 color photos Price Guide 160 pp.
ISBN: 0-7643-1953-1 soft cover $29.95

Imperial Glass: Lace Edge. Laura J. Marsh. A carefully researched guide to Imperial Glass Company's Lace Edge glassware that explains the many variations and compares them to related pieces by Imperial and other manufacturers. Over 325 beautiful color photographs artfully display every documented size and shape and makes it easy for the reader to understand different edges, cuts, intaglio bases, and the subtle variations of more than 40 colors used. With current values in the captions, this book contains all the information collectors need to identify Imperial's Lace Edge glassware.

Size: 8 1/2" x 11" 325 color photos Price Guide 160 pp.
ISBN: 0-7643-2027-0 soft cover $29.95

Elegant Glass with Corn Flower: Imperial Candlewick, Heisey, Tiffin & More. Walter Lemiski. A full color, indispensable identification and price guide for W.J. Hughes's popular Corn Flower pattern designed for Depression Glass and Elegant Glass dealers and collectors. More than 500 images of cherished glassware with accurate values, descriptions, historical information, and identifications from the major American glass works including: Cambridge, Duncan Miller, Fostoria, Heisey, Imperial, Indiana, Jeannette, Lancaster, New Martinsville, Paden City, Tiffin and more, including the Candlewick-Corn Flower connection.

Size: 8 1/2" x 11" 522 color photos Price Guide 160 pp.
ISBN: 0-7643-2141-2 soft cover $29.95

Central Glass Works: The Depression Era. Tim Schmidt. The glassware line produced by Central Glass Works of Wheeling, West Virginia, from the 1910s through 1939, are presented in 470 images. Stemware, tumblers, compotes, marmalades, covered candy dishes, dresser & vanity trays, pitchers, tankards, jugs, candlesticks, & barware appear in many colors, etched decorations, & forms. Values are found both in the captions and in tables.

Size: 8 1/2" x 11" 440 color Price Guide 192 pp.
ISBN: 0-7643-2016-5 soft cover $29.95